Blessed Through the Years

A Compilation of Short Stories and Articles

By

Judith M. Vander Wege

Paperwrights
www.paperwrights.co

How we praise God, the Father of our Lord Jesus Christ,

who has blessed us with every blessing in heaven

because we belong to Christ.

(Ephesians 1:3 LB)

Table of Contents

Chapter one

Sara's Gift, A Response to Love

Sara burst into the house, tears streaming down her cheeks. She slammed the door, then ran upstairs to her room.

"Sara, what …?"

Sara lay face down on her bed, sobbing. She didn't notice her mother come in until she sat down on the bed beside her.

"What's the matter, Honey? What happened?"

Sara gulped her tears as her mother stroked her hair, then caressed her back.

"Nobody likes me," Sara said in a tight voice. She hit the pillow, continuing to sob.

"I like you," her mother said in a soft voice. "So does Daddy."

"Well, Ted sure doesn't," Sara burst out. "He says I can't do anything right."

"Oh, sweetheart. Don't take your brother so seriously. I'm sure he didn't mean it. Now give me a hug before I go finish dinner."

Sara sat up and hugged her mother. She sighed. *Mama doesn't understand how I feel.*

Sara lay back down when her mother left. *They always stick up for Ted. They think he's so perfect! They brag about him and put his school papers and drawings on the frig.*

She turned over and banged on the pillow as the tears flowed again. *And there on the mantel sits his 'amazing' tinker toy creation! He's their favorite for sure…*

2   Sara sat up again, reached for a tissue, and blew her nose…. *just because he can do so many things and isn't scared to tell everyone.* She poked at her stuffed bear, Gris, and told him, "*And every time I want to talk to Mama or Daddy, Ted demands the attention. But since I can't even get good grades or figure out how to make friends, I guess I shouldn't expect them to be proud of me.*" Griz didn't answer. He just looked at her.

At dinner that evening, Sara was even more quiet than usual, as Ted chattered away about school and play.

The next afternoon, mother said, "Sara, will you tell me a story while I fix dinner?"

"Okay, Mama." Sara climbed up on a tall stool beside her. She loved to watch Mama cook. And she loved to make up stories. "June was a ladybug who flew all around the garden…"

"Mother, guess what!" Ted burst through the door, eyes shining. "Oscar wants to teach me how to train horses. He says I'm a natural. But I need my boots. Can you help me find them?

Sara waited while her mother helped Ted. As he dashed out the door, the phone rang. "I'll cut it short, Honey," Mama said. Before Mama finished the phone call, a visitor came. Sara slumped off the stool, trudged up to her bedroom and cried herself to sleep.

In the middle of a dream, she felt a pat on her shoulder. "Sara, Dear, wake up for dinner." Sara could smell the sweet fragrance of floral perfume as her mother bent to kiss her. She opened her eyes and saw she was in her own bed, instead of the flowered meadow of her dream.

That evening after dinner, the scripture Father chose for devotions was about talents. (Matthew 25:14-30.) The King was pleased with two of the people to whom he'd given talents, but he called the third one wicked.

"What are talents?" Ted asked.

"Talents in that day referred to a certain amount of money. The first two used their money wisely, but the third had the wrong attitude and neglected to use his talent."

"Today we think of talents as special abilities or gifts," added Mother.

"Oscar said I have a gift with horses," Ted said, with a smile.

"Why was the third man called wicked?" said Sara.

"Because he didn't use what the king had given him. He just hid it. Whatever gifts we have," Mother said, "God wants us to use them. When we obey, that shows him we love him."

Sara quietly finished her meal. She didn't think she had any gifts. After supper, she went to her room and prayed.

"Dear God, I want to to show you I love you. How can I do that?

The next day was Sunday. Sara loved Sundays because she could go to Sunday School.

Her teacher talked about Jesus feeding the five thousand people, and healing the sick, and blessing the children. Sara asked, "What does Jesus look like?"

Teacher smiled. "Well, there are no actual photographs since they didn't have cameras in those days, but I'm sure his eyes are full of love and understanding. He is happy to see us. His voice is gentle and tender, and he's not in too much of a hurry to talk with us."

Sara felt warm inside. She loved hearing about Jesus.

Another child commented, "I saw a picture of Jesus riding on a donkey. The people waved palm branches and called him a king."

"Yes, Jesus is the King. The Bible calls him the King of Kings and LORD of Lords."

"And he's really alive?" Sara said.

"Yes, he's really alive," Teacher assured her. "And he loves you very much."

When the class ended, most children left quickly, but Sara threw her arms around Teacher in a grateful hug. "My, you seem happy today. Would you like to tell me why?"

"I had a dream about a beautiful King." Sara said.

"Tell me about it," Teacher said, drawing Sara over to a couple chairs to sit down.

Sara told her all about the dream. "The King listened to my stories and told me I have the gift of imagination. Do you think the King could be Jesus?"

"It sounds very much like the way Jesus would act."

"Then I love Jesus and I want to serve him. How can I do that?"

Teacher gave Sara a children's version of the Bible and showed her where she could read about Jesus. "See, in this verse, Jesus said, 'Love one another as I have loved you.' (John15:12). I believe Jesus will be pleased if you use your gift of imagination to show love to people."

All week, Sara read about Jesus in the Bible, and thought of the dream and what her teacher had said. How could she show love? Finally, she had a plan. Saturday morning, Sara put on her clothes and straightened up her room before breakfast. "Would you like me to set the table, Mama?" Her mother looked surprised, then smiled and nodded. After breakfast, Sara helped clear the table, too.

Later, Sara made a card. "Thank you, Mama, for meals, clothes, and everything you do for me and give me." She decorated it with pictures of colored flowers.

"Thank you, Honey. That's very sweet of you." Sara smiled and skipped off happily.

The next afternoon, her dad came in with a quizzical look on his face and a card in his hand. "The car is already washed. And look at this." He showed his wife a card.

A picture of a yellow ice cream cone graced the cover of the card with the words, "Banana-flavored, Yumm." Inside, the first page said, "Thanks for the times you have taken me for rides, stopping to get ice cream or candy."

On the second page it said: "You're the best father a girl ever had … Thanks for being so nice to me, Dad. Love, Sara."

Dad blinked and cleared his throat, then said to Sara, "Now you've got me hungry for one of those cones. Come on, let's go get one."

Later, Sara thought of more ways to show love. She made a card for their sick neighbor and wrote to a lonely aunt. When she heard the little neighbor children fighting, she asked, "Would you like me to tell you a story?"

"Yes," they responded. After the story, they laughed and played.

One day Sara asked her brother, "Ted, will you show me how to play that song Aunt Beth taught you? I'd sure like to play piano like you do."

Surprised, Ted said, "Sure." Over the next few weeks, their relationship improved as Ted taught her what he'd learned. His impatience and criticism often hurt her feelings, but she tried to respond in kindness, as the loving King would like her to respond.

Because she wanted to know King Jesus better, Sara kept reading the Bible. She'd heard the Pastor say it is God's love letter to us. One day at school, she tried to comfort an unhappy friend whose father had moved away. Sara told her, "The Bible says God will never leave us nor forsake us. "For God loved the world so much he gave his only Son …""

This friend came with her to Sunday School the following Sunday. When Sara talked with the teacher afterwards, she told Sara, "See. You used your gift of imagination to show love, and now she wants a close relationship with Jesus like you have."

Thank you, King Jesus," Sara prayed silently. "*The greatest gift of all is to share your love.*"

Chapter Tow

Sierra Builds a Bridge

"Sierra Rose. Yes, I'll name her Sierra Rose," Samantha whispered. She clasped her hands to her chest. Standing on the lower log of a split rail fence, she watched her birthday present trot around the corral. With her arms on the top log, she gazed at the beautiful filly. *She's exactly the color of rosewood from Sierra Leone, like that elegant furniture in the encyclopedia, reddish brown with black streaks.*

Samantha imagined the rhythm of the horse's hooves saying, "Happy birthday." As the breeze played with her long, black hair, Samantha wished she could stay with her horse rather than go to school. Her smile faded. *Why is middle school so frustrating? Why can't I make friends?*

As if to comfort her, the filly came close.

"Good morning, Sierra Rose," she murmured, stroking the velvety nose while giving her a carrot. "At least *you'll* have a good morning, just running around a nice pasture and eating. I have to recite a poem in front of the whole class!"

Samantha poured grain into a pail, brushed the filly's glossy coat, and practiced her poem. "I love you when … "

She boarded the bus, dreading fourth period.

Later, Samantha tried to listen to the others recite. Then … "Samantha. Didn't you hear me? I said it is your turn. Please come up now." Samantha slowly walked to the front. She saw all those eyes facing her. Soon the whole room seemed to sway. She tried to focus but couldn't remember what to do. Everything seemed blurry. She opened her mouth, but no words came out. She looked imploringly at the teacher, tears welling up in her eyes.

"OK, sit down." Mrs. Harrington sighed. "Stay and talk with me after class, please."

"You need to conquer your shyness," she told Samantha later. "Half of your grade depends on these presentations. If you can't recite, you'll receive an F." Samantha's throat tightened. If she got an F, her mother would ground her from her horse.

Rushing into fifth period, Samantha heard Alicia whisper, "Hi, 'fraidy cat." Other kids snickered. She didn't recognize them; all the faces at this new school blurred together.

Throughout the next week, Samantha worked on the next English assignment, a five-paragraph essay. *I could get an A if I just didn't have to read it to the class.* She practiced it while she rode Sierra Rose and brushed her. The day before the assignment was due, Sierra pricked up her ears and nudged her shoulder as if to say, "That's my girl. You can do it."

The day of the oral presentation, Samantha woke with a stomachache. "Please, let me stay home, Mom," she begged. Her mother refused.

During fourth period, she lay down in the health room, then took her health room pass and the written essay to her teacher. Next day her teacher said, "Samantha, this is an excellent essay. Will you read it to the class today?" Samantha shook her head, feeling her stomachache return.

"I'll give you a few days. Let me know when you're ready." Samantha nodded. She had it memorized, but couldn't get up in front of that classroom again.

Next, the class had two weeks to practice plays, Samantha heard Jennie whisper to Alicia,"Wish we didn't have 'fraidy cat in our group."

"Yeah," Alicia said. "She'll probably mess up our whole play."

Samantha read her lines so softly in the group they could hardly hear her. But she read them loudly to her horse each evening. Soon she knew the entire play by memory

The day they were to give the play, Samantha's stomach hurt again. But she was determined not to fail her group. In their costumes, they gathered at the front of the class. But when it came time for her to say her lines, she froze. *They're all staring at me! What am I supposed to say?* She clapped her hand over her mouth, ran out and threw up in the restroom.

On the bus that afternoon, Samantha pondered her problem. She prayed for help.

Later, after riding, Samantha brushed down her horse. "What am I going to do, Sierra? I have to recite in front of the class to get a passing grade. I'll never be able to do it."

Sierra gave her a sympathetic whinny.

"Thanks. I never forget my lines when I'm talking to you."She held the brush in midair-- "Hey. I have an idea." She quickly fed Sierra Rose and ran to the house.

"Mom, I have an idea!"

"Hello, Dear." Mom called. "I baked your favorite cookies." Mom set a plate of cookies and a glass of milk on the table, then sat down as if waiting to talk with her.

Samantha joined her. Looking into her mother's smiling face, Samantha shared her idea.

"Why, that's a wonderful idea, if they'll let you do it."

The next morning, Samantha went to Mrs. Harrington before school. "I have an idea how to do the oral assignments," she began, shyly.

"Good. Let's hear it."

"I practice reciting with my horse all the time. So I wonder if the class could take a field trip to our farm."

Her teacher smiled. "Hmm. That would be highly unusual, but interesting. I'll see what the principal says." Later, she told her the good news, "We can do it next week." The day of the field trip dawned bright and sunny. When they arrived, the teacher announced, "This farm belongs to Samantha's family. She has something special to show you. And this," she said as the bus door opened, "is her mother, Mrs. Benavides."

After the children said hello, Samantha led them to the corral. "Wait here," she whispered to the teacher, who motioned to the class. She whistled softly and Sierra Rose came running. Samantha fed her a piece of apple and caressed her nose. Then she climbed on the fence and spoke softly. The horse came close enough for Samantha to climb onto her bare back. Alicia and Jenny whispered and giggled, but the kids around them told them to shush.

Samantha beckoned the students to come closer. They gathered on the fence and Samantha began her essay. "Sierra Rose, my two-year-old Morgan filly, is my favorite pet." She patted the horse's neck, occasionally looking up at her audience. She remembered every word and her voice became stronger as she continued. She concluded, saying, "Beautiful Sierra Rose has a pleasant personality, and is strong and capable. She is my favorite pet."

The students clapped and some cheered. Samantha and Sierra Rose galloped once around the corral. When they stopped in front of the class, Samantha slid off over the tail. Mom handed Samantha a carrot, who fed it to Sierra Rose. The teacher motioned for the class to be quiet as Samantha began reciting her poem to her beloved horse, while caressing her velvety nose. She finished, "… and the reason why I love you is just because you're you." She hugged
Sierra Rose around the neck. The class clapped again. With a smile, the teacher said, "All right, Samantha, I think you've succeeded in bringing your grade up.

"That calls for a celebration," Mom said. "Come over to the yard for some homemade donuts and milk."

While eating, Samantha and her play group finalized plans. Then they walked back to the corral and stood around Sierra Rose while acting out their play. They adjusted it a little to include a horse. Samantha felt so happy, sharing her best friend with her new friends, that she forgot to be nervous.

Sierra Rose, a horse the color of rare and precious wood, "built a bridge" that day for a shy girl to cross over into friendship and success.

Chapter Three

Someone who cares

Trina entered her empty house and dropped her book bag by the kitchen table. *I'm so sick of those long, lonely bus rides.* She grabbed the saltines and butter, and sat down to read the newspaper comics. Eating buttered crackers seemed to help somehow.

I don't see why no one wants to sit with me. But then, if my own mother doesn't feel like talking with me, why should anyone else? I must be awfully boring.

Trina pushed her long brown hair back from her face and wiped her eyes with a napkin. She gave up trying to enjoy the "funnies" and took out her homework, trying to push aside the remembrance of the evening before. After finally working up the courage to ask her mother for advice, her mother had said, "Not now, dear. I've got to call Cynthia first."

Knowing the phone call would take awhile, Trina had gone upstairs to do homework. *Maybe Mom will come up and talk later.* But she didn't. When Trina went down later to say goodnight, both parents were already in bed, sound asleep.

They work so hard, it's no wonder they're tired. But I still felt gypped.

Trina buttered another cracker. *I'll try again tonight.* She finished her math homework in half an hour, then opened her English book. Looking at the clock, she sighed. *I better start supper soon. I'll read just a couple pages first.* But the story captured her attention and, before she knew it, her mother walked in the door.

"Do you mean you haven't even started supper?" Mother stood in the kitchen with a pained look on her face.

"I'm sorry, Mom. I got carried away reading the story for English." Trina quickly cleared the table of her homework.

"Well, it seems you get carried away too often," Mother said. "It seems like you spend most of your life in a fantasy land."

So, is it wrong to read my English assignment? Trina wanted to retort, but she didn't dare. Fantasy did seem more fulfilling than real life. She tried to start supper, but her mother pushed her aside. "Don't bother now. I can do it faster myself. Just set the table."

Trina felt worse than ever. Why was she even born? When her dad came home, he bawled her out for not carrying out her responsibilities. Supper had such a tense atmosphere, the food didn't even taste good.

After Trina meekly washed the dishes, she approached her mother again, and asked, "Please, Mom, can I talk to you about something?"

"Trina," her dad said in his irritated voice, "you know your mother is tired after working ten hour days. Then she had to cook supper, too, thanks to your neglect. Just leave her alone now, and let her rest."

As the tears welled from deep inside, Trina turned and ran out the back door, slamming it as hard as she could. She ran across the back yard to the river, climbed her favorite tree, and sat there sobbing. *If I were a mom or dad, I would go after my child and talk about what's bothering her.* She wiped her eyes. *It must be my own fault they won't talk with me. I must not be lovable enough.*

After several minutes, she remembered something she'd been told at Bible Camp: "Jesus loves you and wants to be your friend. You can talk to him anytime." Maybe it was worth a try.

"Jesus, did you make a mistake when you made me? Why doesn't anyone care to talk to me?" Trina listened, but didn't hear any answer. Yet, she felt a little less lonely while talking to him. Soon she had the urge to write a poem. She dug out the paper and pencil stashed in a hole in her tree, and wrote:

I *sit here alone, wishing for something I can't describe.*

Wishing I could pour out my feelings to someone who cares, but no one does.

Yet, they tell me you care. Do you, Jesus?

They tell me you once felt a little like I do now: Hurt, rejected, abandoned.

Trina gazed at the river flowing peacefully below, and remembered a song they'd sung at camp: "I've got a river of life flowing out of me." She wanted it to be true. Ever since returning home three months earlier, she had missed the peace and joy she'd felt at camp. They had told her that this "river of life" was the Holy Spirit and that he would flow out of her if only she completely surrendered her life to Jesus. Now, she wanted to do that.

"Jesus, I'm sorry for not doing this earlier. I now surrender myself to you. I want you to do your will in my life. Fill me with your Holy Spirit and teach me how to have your kind of attitudes." In the next few minutes, she was amazed at the feeling of peace which came over her. After enjoying this feeling a few minutes, she completed her poem.

Yes, of course you care. You cared enough to die for me.

You care enough to intercede for me.

"By your stripes I have been healed" and you sent your Holy Spirit

to comfort me, guide me, and be with me forever.

Thank you, Lord.

Trina climbed down and returned to the house. She wondered how the "River of Life" would flow out of her, now that she had surrendered to Jesus. A feeling of love and peace filled her heart as she entered the door. "Forgive me, Lord, for slamming the door so hard. Bless my parents and help them get enough rest."

She found her parents in the living room, Dad sound asleep and Mom reading a magazine. "Mom, could I get you anything?"

"Why, yes, Dear; a mug of hot milk would be nice."

"With cinnamon?"

"Yes, please."

Trina brought the hot milk and set it on the stand near her mother, then sat down near her.

Mother took a sip, then said, "Thank you. Now what was it you wanted to talk with me about last evening when I got busy with that phone call?"

"Well..." Trina cleared her throat. "I'm having trouble making friends in high school. I thought you might have some ideas."

Mother looked thoughtful. "I had that problem, too, when I was your age." She smiled at Trina. "One thing that might help: someone told me once that a smile is a great friendship-starter. So I began smiling at everyone I met, and it did help.

"The most important thing is, once you start talking with someone, be more concerned about that person than yourself. Let your interest show and listen with eye contact, perhaps asking questions about what they're saying. This makes it easier for the person to talk, and hopefully they'll reciprocate with interest in you."

Trina listened intently. It sounded like good advice. "Thank you, Mom. I'll try that. Goodnight now. I love you."

"I love you, too, dear. Goodnight."

Chapter Four

A Ticket Fiasco

From the day I'd first seen our new neighbor, Lily, I'd wanted to be her special friend, maybe even take her to the prom. Butch said, "Dream on, buddy. Better find someone your own skin color!" We are all in the same Sunday School class so, ignoring Butch, I'd asked Lily if I could give her a ride to the bus the day of the culture day trip and she readily agreed.

The day started out great. I picked up our bus tickets from school, then rode my scooter to her house. "Good morning, Lily," I said. "We should make it to the Greyhound station in plenty of time for the ten o'clock departure."

We knew something was wrong when we walked into the nearly empty station. *Where are our classmates? We were all supposed to ride the same bus.* Swallowing the lump in my throat, I asked at the ticket booth. His answer felt like a club hitting me in the chest. "That bus left at 9."

I stared at him numbly, then dug out our tickets and stared at them. "Uh oh!"

"What's the matter, Antonio?" Lily asked.

I looked into her sweet, blue eyes. How could I deliver this blow? "The bus left at nine."

"Oh no! You told me ten." (She'd been absent the day we got the bus announcement.)

"I know. I'm so sorry."

Lily crossed her arms and tapped her foot. "So what do we do now?"

I studied the tickets, hoping they'd change their minds. *Oh God! What should I do?*

We found a bench nearby and sat down. I could feel her irritation. It burned a hole in my dreams. So much for friendship.

"There's no way we could catch that bus with your scooter."

"No. I'm not even allowed to take the scooter out on the highway."

Lily leaned back against the wall, sighing. "I suppose we'll get an F since we won't be able to do this assignment." She sounded defeated.

"Yeah." I kicked a pebble away.

"No, wait a minute!" I turned to her, feeling lit up like a light-bulb.

Startled, Lily jumped up.

"Lily, what exactly did the assignment say?"

With a puzzled look, she quoted: "Write a paper about the differences between two cultures."

"That's all, right?"

"Yes."

"OK. So the busload is going to a museum which has a Black History display and a Hispanic display. We can't experience the culture the way the rest of the class will. But you and I have our own two cultures. You're Caucasian-American and I'm African-

American. We can interview each other and go to the library. If we write good papers, we should get good grades."

Lily's eyes lit up like a sunrise. "We can also look at that display at the tea shop—some paintings of black people and some of white."

"I don't remember seeing that."

"They just put it up recently in honor of Martin Luther King Day and Presidents' Day."

We did a high-five and picked up our backpacks.

"Let's go to the tea shop first. We can look at the paintings, then sit in a booth and write our impressions…."

"then interview each other over lunch," she added, eyes shining.

Alright, I thought. *Maybe this day will turn out better than I thought a few minutes ago.*

Suddenly, Lily turned around as we walked out the door, bumping into me. I knocked my head on the door frame and nearly fell.

"Oh-oh, Sorry! I just thought….Since we can't use the bus tickets, can you get a refund?"

I rubbed my head. "Good idea. Lunch money." I went to the ticket desk and had to wait several minutes, but finally got a refund.

At the tea shop, I parked the scooter and we went in.

"What differences do you notice in these pictures?" I asked, pointing to two.

"They dress a little differently, don't they?"

"Yes, but I think these are depicting scenes from a couple hundred years ago. Do you see that much difference now?"

"No. 'Course, we are both Americans."

In a booth, after ordering lunch, we interviewed each other. "Holiday traditions? Family relationships?"

After discussing these and other questions, we discovered something. Since we both came from Christian families, we had more similarities than differences.

After lunch, we went to the Public Library and asked the Librarian for help on finding information about cultures. We checked into dances, celebrations, clothes, attitudes toward relatives, and several other things.

"I think we have enough material to write good papers, don't you, Lily?"

"Yes. We should go now."

At Lily's house later, she said, "Thanks, Antonio. I had a lot of fun and we solved our problem together. You've become a good friend today."

As she went inside, I smiled and pumped my fist in the air.

Chapter five

A Friend-Maker Game

Standing at the edge of the playground, I looked at the crowd of kids and felt lost.

The bus ride on this, my first day of school, had felt okay because my older sister rode with me. But when we arrived at the huge school, she disappeared. The first-grade classroom held more children than I'd ever seen before.

Now, at the edge of the playground at recess, I felt all alone and scared. It seemed there were hundreds of children. *What was I supposed to do? How do kids start playing with kids they don't know?* At age six, I hadn't had much opportunity to play with other children except my big sister and my baby sister. I felt overwhelmed.

Then a big girl named Stella came up to me and asked, "Would you like to play jacks?"

Jacks? What's that? I wondered, but I nodded. Grateful for something to do, I followed her to a secluded, shady spot on the sidewalk.

"My name is Stella. I'm in third grade." She showed me a small ball and ten little metal things she had in her hand. "These are jacks." Then she spread out the metal things on the sidewalk.

"Okay. This is what you do." She bounced the small ball once, and while it was in the air she quickly picked up one jack. Then she caught the ball before it hit the sidewalk. "That's onesies."

Stella was a third-grader. She could do this. She bounced the ball again and again, each time picking up a jack until she had all ten of them. "Now you try."

I bounced the ball. It bounced away onto the dirt, and my uncoordinated hands picked up nothing. I guessed she won the "onesies."

"Okay, now it's my turn again."

I watched carefully as Stella bounced the ball and quickly picked up two jacks. She repeated this until she had picked up all ten. Then she handed them to me. "Now you try it."

I tried and tried until finally I began to be successful. By the time recess was over, I became excited about the game. Every recess for a while thereafter, I looked for Stella and we had fun together playing jacks, from onesies to twosies and all the way to tens.

Later, I had the confidence to play on the playground equipment, when I didn't see Stella.

I'm so glad Stella asked me to play this friend-maker game. It was a simple thing, but her invitation to play jacks made a great difference in my adjustment to school.

If you like to play Jacks, or some other simple game, perhaps you can find some scared, lonely person to play with. You can be a blessing, maybe even a hero or heroine, to that person. You might even make a friend.

Adult Short Stories (Fiction)

Chapter Six

Desire of My Heart

Jolted out of a sound sleep, Bethanne reached across the bed's empty space to turn off the jangling alarm clock. Sunshine streamed through the window. The curtains swayed gently in the breeze. The realization hit her again: *He's not just traveling this time. He's dead! Maurice won't be coming back.*

Aren't you used to it yet? Bethanne mumbled to herself. *It's been two years! But then, we were married forty.*

Going through the motions of bathing and dressing, Bethanne pushed aside the lonely feelings. It seemed as if she had always been alone, deep down inside, even when Maurice was alive.

Bethanne sat at the table with a peach, toast and her Bible. She read listlessly until noticing John 10:10. Tearfully, she prayed, "Lord Jesus, thank you for eternal life. I have entered by you, the Door. But I feel so lonely, as if a thief has stolen the abundant life I should have. Please, … help me?" She sat silently a few moments, wishing God would speak to her audibly.

Then, to her surprise, a face came to her mind. With the face came a feeling, inexplicably, of hope—of happy expectation. Where had she seen this man? He looked to be about her age, with charcoal hair streaked with silver. *Oh, yes! He taught at my school one day last year. As I left the staff room after lunch, he passed me coming in. As our eyes met, my heart fluttered like crazy. I was so flustered I didn't even say hello but just hurried to the music room. There I fanned my hot face and thought, guiltily, My beloved husband has been gone little more than a year, and I'm getting heart flutters for another man?*

Bethanne hadn't seen the substitute teacher since, and was too embarrassed to ask anyone who he was. Her first impression was that he seemed kind, gentle, understanding, and strong. Could he be the soul-mate she longed for?

Bethanne chided herself. How could she form that much of an impression from one glance? *Ridiculous!* She forced herself to turn her attentions to the day ahead. She loved teaching music at Pervins Elementary. *Children are so quick to love anyone who spends happy times with them,* she thought. *And what better happy times than in making music?* The children comforted her.

But lunchtime was often difficult. Other teachers conversed about their husbands and families. "We went on a trip to Victoria Island," exulted one. "After the kids won their baseball game, we …"

"... The championship tennis match reminded us of when we met."

"On our anniversary," said another, "Georgie surprised me with a trip to Seattle, a romantic dinner and dance."

Bethanne couldn't even remember similar happy times with her husband. He'd gone fishing or hunting with his friends, while she did the weekend housework. She'd taught full-time, and had cared for their son until he left home. Her social life consisted of choir practice and Bible Studies.

But at least, then, her husband was part of her life. She missed his "Good morning, Babe; how did you sleep?" She missed fixing his coffee and lunch in the mornings, folding his clothes, having dinner ready when he got home from work. Oh, sure, it was easier not to have to cope with the arguing when they disagreed about financial decisions and religious matters. It was a relief to no longer have to worry about his drinking when he went to the tavern to play pool. Sometimes her heart still ached at the memory of his neglect of her. At times, she had thought it would be more peaceful and comfortable living alone. But now she missed him.

I miss being needed, she admitted to herself. *I miss scratching his back at bedtime and massaging his neck. I miss praying for him; it's too late to pray for him now. I hope God got through to him at the last minute. Her* biggest fear was that he hadn't.

Bethanne got up with a sigh and took her dish to the sink. *Thank you, Lord, that at least I don't have financial worries. Maurice was a good worker and earned a good pension.*

It was time to leave for school. Bethanne's favorite class was at the end of the day. But then it would be time to go home to an empty house. That was the worst. Maurice used to watch TV while Bethanne did housework. It had been a form of togetherness. At times they would check on each other and exchange a bit of small talk. Maybe they'd even go for a walk together.

Bethanne sighed as she put on her jacket. She left for school, firmly shutting the door on both house and emotions.

That noon, her friend, Elena, greeted her cheerfully. "Come and have lunch with me outside." Bethanne smiled and followed her. As they enjoyed the gentle spring breeze, sitting on a bench next to blooming daffodils, Elena asked, "What are you doing this evening, Bethanne?"

Bethanne glanced at her, then stared off into the distance. "Rattling around in an empty house, wishing I were back at work."

Elena looked at her sympathetically. "You sound lonely. Isn't it about time you get a social life?"

"I am lonely," admitted Bethanne. "But at my age, where would I start?"

"Have you ever tried Old Time Fiddlers?" asked Elena.

"I've heard of it, but I don't play the fiddle."

"You're so musical, you probably could. But they play other instruments, also. Don't you play a guitar and an accordion?"

"It's a mandolin, and yes, an accordion and piano."

"Perfect!" Elena exclaimed. "Hey, let's go to the potluck and jam on Saturday. I've been itching to play my harmonica."

That Saturday evening as she and Elena walked into the school gymnasium, Bethanne worried. *Why did I let her talk me into this? I don't like crowds of people I don't know.* She saw a long table along one side where people kept setting more dishes of food. "Salads go here," Elena said. They set their dishes down, then brought in Bethanne's mandolin and accordion.

Several people played music in the corner for a few minutes until someone announced, "Time to eat." In the food line, Elena introduced her to several people. By the time they ate, Bethanne felt at ease. After eating, most of them went to the other end of the gymnasium and either played music together or watched. Soon she was laughing and tapping her feet.

"This is the most fun I've had in a long time!" Bethanne whispered to Elena during a break.

"Great!" responded her friend. "And did you notice any handsome, available men?"

Bethanne blushed. "I'm not looking for any."

Elena grinned, "Well, I am. Of course, I've been widowed much longer than you have.

Thomas and Vincent are sure good-looking, aren't they? Thomas is a widower and Vincent is a bachelor," she whispered.

Bethanne watched the ones she pointed out during the next part of the jam session. She had to admit, they were good-looking. Her interest increased as she noticed their musical abilities. Vincent sang and played a string bass. *What a card!* She thought, watching his antics. Sometimes he waltzed with his bass, sometimes rode it like a horse, or played it while lying on the floor. The audience loved it and Bethanne laughed 'til her jaw hurt.

The following month, Bethanne was eager to attend the Old Time Fiddler's potluck and jam, and get better acquainted with the group. Could she start dating again? She searched her heart, wondering if she was ready. Would Vincent be a good companion? But she lost interest in him when he played and sang raunchy songs, and then went out for a smoke. *Not soul-mate material for me, she thought.*

Bethanne turned her attention to Thomas, and she liked what she saw and heard. He could make that fiddle sing, and was the most handsome man she had ever met. "A bunch of us are going out to coffee," he told her when the jam was over. "Do you want to come?"

Bethanne enjoyed conversing with Thomas and the rest at the restaurant. She felt they were "clicking." He invited her out to dinner the following weekend and she eagerly said "yes." The dinner date was all she'd hoped for, leaving Bethanne on cloud nine for days.

For the next six months, Thomas and Bethanne kept missing connections for one reason or another. She began to think this relationship wasn't meant to be. Meanwhile, Bethanne's relationship with God grew more intimate. Thinking of Psalm 37:4, she asked God, "Please give me the desire of my heart for a soul-mate. But more than that, LORD, I desire to live in tune with you." When she went out with Thomas again, his conversation seemed boring and his values weak.

Bethanne decided to volunteer her music at the Sunrise Nursing Home once a week, playing and singing mostly gospel songs. "They sure love your music," the activity director told her, "and so do their visitors."

She looked forward to these times. Tired eyes lit up when they saw her. Alzheimer patients who didn't even remember their own names sang along on the old hymns. They would tell her "Thank you so much for coming," or "That was … delicious!" or "I haven't heard those wonderful songs in so long!"

After a few weeks at Sunrise, Bethanne discovered a precious depth to her relationship with God. She felt she was one of God's instruments. *This is it, isn't it, LORD? This relationship with you is the abundant life!* She felt happier than ever before. Widowhood wasn't so bad after all.

Shortly after this, Bethanne noticed that a resident whom she had grown to love had a visitor. Mrs. Warren, a sweet lady who often expressed appreciation of her music, came into the room holding hands with a handsome gentleman while Bethanne sang "The Rose." As she finished, she got a glimpse of his face and her heart jumped to her throat. *It's him! The one who subbed at school, whose face came to my mind when I prayed about my loneliness. So that's Mrs. Warren's husband!* Her face felt hot, and she requested a glass of ice water. After the program, she hurried out without her usual greetings.

The next week, Bethanne was sick. The following week, she felt like canceling again at Sunrise, but decided that wasn't fair. *Since this ministry is my offering to God, I shouldn't stay away just because some guy makes me feel uncomfortable. It isn't fair to him, either, or to his lovely wife.*

During the music that day, Mrs. Warren's face shone. "I'm so glad you're back!" she said. After the music, she insisted Bethanne stay for lunch and sit with them. "This is my brother, Russell Jeremiah Andreisen," she said proudly, as Bethanne reached their table. Her love was evident in her voice and smile.

"Your brother!" Bethanne exclaimed, dropping her purse.

"Yes; I'm happy to meet you," he said, after picking up her purse. "Thanks for granting my request to sing "The Rose" again. I've loved that song, especially since my wife died five years ago. You sing it beautifully." He pulled out the chair for her and motioned for her to sit down.

Bethanne had no idea, afterward, what she ate for lunch that day. But she learned Russell's deep blue eyes twinkled, and crinkled on the outer edges when he talked. His voice sounded like a soothing stream. He was a deeply devoted Christian, a retired English teacher, and he loved music.

"I'd love to play music here with you sometime," he said. "I play a mouth organ and guitar. How about it?"

"We could practice and see how it goes," Bethanne said.

They practiced a few days later in Bethanne's living room. They loved many of the same gospel songs and had a wonderful time playing and singing together for three hours.

"Wow, look at the time," Russell said. "It sure went fast." He got up to put away his guitar while Bethanne got out some cookies and lemonade.

They sat at the table to eat. A few minutes later, Russell said softly, "It's time for me to go now. Would you pray with me first?" Bethanne nodded and he took her hand. Bethanne's heart raced as he spoke intimately with their loving Father. She wished they would never have to part. She felt like part of her left with him when they'd said goodbye.

Several months later, after many dates of music or dinner, hiking or church events, Russell brought Bethanne to a beautiful rose garden on a sunny day. "I've been wanting to bring you here ever since you sang "The Rose," he said, smiling tenderly. He picked a deep burgundy rose and handed it to her.

He guided her to a bench in front of lovely flowers. After sitting silently for a few moments, he turned to her and said, "I wrote a poem I'd like you to read. But first I want to say something, to ask you something. And before you answer, please read the poem.

"It has been wonderful spending time with you," he continued. Bethanne's throat constricted. He seemed so serious. Was he preparing to tell her they shouldn't see each other any more?

Russell looked away and stood up, as if he didn't know how to start. "We have hit it off like kindred spirits," he said softly, looking at her with smiling eyes. "I almost feel as if we are soul-mates already." Bethanne's heart lurched. Russell sat down next to her and took her hand.

Using his pet name for her, he said, "Bethany, if we marry, I believe we will be true soul-mates. Please, would you read this poem and then tell me you will consider marrying me?"

Bethanne couldn't speak. She felt like she was falling into the warm pool of Russell's eyes, being bathed by the love in them. She took the paper and read:

Bethany

The moon-light shining on the placid lake

is like your presence reflecting on my heart.

Together we create a scene of peace.

May the One who has created us both

be glorified in our shining, our togetherness.

May the Prince of Peace unite us as one.

---By Russell

She read slowly and silently, tears of joy and gratitude to God filling her eyes. As she looked up into Russell's eyes, he said, "I love you, Bethany. Will you marry me?" She smiled joyfully through her tears, nodding yes. As they embraced, she thought she could hear angels singing. Or was that her own heart praising God? He had granted the desire of her heart.

Chapter Seven

Loosed from the shackles

Evergreens decked with snow guarded the lighted farmhouse. Geese flew in formation, silhouetted by the sunset sky. Four children played in the yard, guarded by their snowman. Across the pond, a few mallards slept while others stood watch on Christmas Eve, 2003, the lull before the storm.

Lil glanced at her whistling husband. *Nearly sixteen years with this wonderful man.* "It's almost time for Gene and Peggy to arrive." Lil stepped to the door, "Kids, come in and get ready."

Four giggling children trooped in: Andrew, Christina, Olaf, and Peachy. They took off boots and coats while Jeff teased them.

A sliver of fear shot through Lil. What would she do if anything happened? Her family was her life.

After a wonderful meal and time with their friends, Lil relished spending a few moments with Jeff. As they packed his suitcase, she proudly remembered his boss's words: "Jeff has been chosen to take the company's expansion plans to the headquarters back east. After all, most of the ideas were his. This is a great honor."

Closing the suitcase, she wondered why Jeff was so quiet. He walked around slowly, looking at pictures on the walls, looking out the window at the garden and fields on their tiny farm, or watching her work.

But next morning, he gave her his usual grin. "I'll see you later," he said, as he hugged her goodbye.

Jeff drove his pickup to the train station. He phoned every evening and said the meetings went well. The day Jeff was to return, a blizzard hit the area. Lil expected him at midnight.

While cleaning and baking his favorite pie, she kept looking out the window. A terrible fear gripped her heart.

What if he's dead ... and not coming back? The storm outside seemed minor compared to the storm within her heart.

After what seemed an eternity, the dreaded knock came. A policeman. "I'm sorry, Mrs. Prescott. The train was derailed in the blizzard."

An emotional avalanche hit Lil's lungs and she struggled to breathe. The policeman caught her as she tottered and guided her to a chair. He squatted beside her, then gently explained, "Jeff was thrown out during the wreck. His head hit a rock. He was killed instantly."

Lil screamed, "No-o-o!"

She wept and shivered, dimly aware the children had awakened and come downstairs. The policeman gathered the four together and told them the news. They cried and ran to their mother. She tried to hug them but felt numb.

The next week was a daze. She went through the motions of plans and funeral.

During the next months, Lil felt as if she had a hole in her chest. *Life goes on, but do I have to?* She plodded through the "necessities" of life. Gone was the joy of their peaceful setting, the smell of cookies, children's laughter, Jeff's whistles, his voice whispering love.

"How could he do it?" She shouted at her friend, Peggy. "God is supposed to be love. But he took away the love of my life!"

Peggy hugged her silently, then murmured, "God wants to be the love of your life."

With their grief ignored, the children exhibited signs of inner chaos. Third quarter report cards showed failing grades for Olaf and Peachy. Christina acted like an alien. Andrew finished driver's education, earned his license, then got arrested for a DWI.

Lil was forced to see their pain. "What can I do?" she asked Peggy. "How can I keep my kids from self-destruction when I can barely manage to get dressed in the morning?"

Peggy hugged Lil. "Help is available. I know a family counselor who can help you and your children through this valley."

Lil and her children began sessions with Mrs. Denton, a Biblical counselor. The children benefited immediately. They were hungry to talk to someone. "I think we're hurting as much as Mom," Andrew said. "But she's in her own world. She doesn't smile anymore. She doesn't even cook like she used to. It's almost like it's our fault."

"I'm scared," Christina admitted. "My dad is dead, and my mom is going crazy. I don't know what to do."

When Mrs. Denton talked to Peachy, she cried out, "I want my daddy!"

Olaf wouldn't speak. He looked at the counselor with pleading eyes and scooted close to her on the couch.

"What can I do?" Lil asked. "I didn't realize they were hurting so much. But I feel like mush. How can I help my children when I have nothing to give?"

"You can't. You need supernatural help. I don't have all the answers, but I have one. Do you personally know Jesus Christ?"

"We haven't been going to church. It's too much of an effort to go to town. Jeff used to read us a Bible Story on Sundays."

"Jesus Christ can help you and your children, if you'll let him," Mrs. Denton said.

Lil sat quietly. *That's easy for you to say. You haven't lost your husband.*

Mrs. Denton softly told her "My husband died a few years ago. If it hadn't been for my relationship with Christ, I would have committed suicide."

Lil burst into tears and her anger evaporated.

That evening Lil began to read Jeff's Bible. On the bookmark, Jeff had written. "You shall know the truth and the truth shall set you free." She repeated it several times, pondering its meaning.

Am I not free? The truth came into focus. *I haven't trusted Christ to be in charge of my life. I've been shackled by unbelief!* Lil found other verses Jeff had underlined, promises of God's love. Then she remembered his last words to her, "I'll see you later."

She prayed, "I'm sorry, Lord Jesus. Please forgive me for being angry with you, for not trusting you. Forgive me for thinking only of my pain. Please help my children. Help me be the mother they need. Forgive me for not believing your love. Thank you I will see my husband again in Heaven."

The next day, Lil gathered the children together and asked them to forgive her for being selfish. They hugged and cried together.

The world began to seem brighter. They read the Bible and prayed together often, drawing closer. Gradually, the grief subsided. An inner joy began to glimmer.

A few months later, Lil gave her testimony in church. "I didn't think I needed God. I just needed my husband and family, our peaceful world. It took a train wreck to shake me loose from the shackles of unbelief. My husband's death threw me into a deep depression. I was angry with God. How dare he take away the love of my life! It was so frightening! I felt there was no use living anymore.

"For a while, I thought of ways to kill myself. But when the children began getting into trouble, I realized I had to snap out of this mood and help them. Then I was even more desperate! How could I help them when I had nothing to give?

"That's when the Lord Jesus began to teach me the truth about how to surrender to him. Relationship with Him is the answer. He is the truth. He set me free. He loosed me from the shackles."

Chapter Eight

Christmas Again!

"Christmas again," Dorine mumbled, staring out the window. Huge snowflakes fluttered down. Such a sight used to fill her heart with gladness. Now she struggled against the darkness threatening to engulf her.

Sighing, she picked a gray hair off her baggy black sweater. How could she possibly handle Christmas preparations this year?

Christmas used to be my favorite time of year. Pete would come in covered with snow, laughing as the children crowded past him eager to tell me, "Mommy, look! We got a tree--- Daddy chopped it down!"

Dorine turned from the window and slumped into a chair, continuing her reverie. *Lisa and Kirk unwrapped decorations with giggles and hung them in clumps on the tree. The house was filled with love as we decorated the house and baked cookies together. The children made each day seem like a gift. Life was simpler. Peaceful.*

What happened? Why?

Dorine dragged herself into the kitchen to wash dishes. A scene from five years ago became vivid: Lisa, who'd married right after high school, was spending this last Christmas at home before moving across the nation with her military husband. "Mom," Lisa asked, setting the Christmas centerpiece on the table, "where's Dad?"

"Oh, I'm sure he'll be here soon, dear. He's probably doing some last minute shopping." Dorine lifted her best china out of the hutch, thinking of Pete's complaint a week earlier. "Guess these kids don't need us anymore, now that Lisa's married and Kirk has his driver's license. He's too busy to even go skiing with me."

Kirk, indeed, seldom spent time with his parents anymore, but for good reasons. His car wash job, track events, school, and friends took up most of his time. However, that Christmas Eve was to be a special time with the whole family together. Dorine looked forward to getting better acquainted with their new son-in-law, too.

It's not like Pete to be late. Where is he? She forced a smile onto her face.

Soon they had the table beautifully decorated, the turkey dinner ready to be dished up, but Pete wasn't home yet. They turned the oven and burners on warm, then sat down to visit.

An hour later, the phone rang. "Honey, I'm shorry, can't make it for dinner, havin' a few drinks witha guys. You go head'n eat."

Dorine stared in disbelief at the phone as she heard a click and dial tone. *How could he?* She took a deep breath and told them, "He can't come, he's busy with some associates," Their joy was dampened, but hunger took precedence over disappointment and they managed to enjoy the evening with each other.

Doreen wiped her hands and eyes on the dishtowel. *But, for me, something began to die that night. Hours later, when Pete stumbled in and fell into bed beside me, I almost threw up from the smell. When I said goodbye to Lisa and Jack in the morning,*

Lisa asked about her dad. I simply said he had late business and arrived home dead tired.

Each Christmas since, Pete got drunk. The kids never saw, and I didn't tell them. It wouldn't help to worry them. In the summer when they came for brief visits, he seemed okay. Doreen alone saw the problem worsen. *How long before he loses his job or has a car wreck or something?*

She urged him to go for counseling or to AA. But he couldn't see that his drinking was a problem. "I can control it. I still have my job, don't I? I haven't hurt anyone."

But it did hurt someone. It hurt her --- deep down inside where no one could see. She no longer enjoyed him as her soul mate. He seemed a stranger with whom she didn't feel comfortable. They couldn't have meaningful conversations because of disagreements. She couldn't invite company over, never knowing if he would be home and sober. And how could she trust him, knowing how alcohol can influence a person?

Dorine bade her reverie to stop. *It's hopeless. There's no reason to decorate or bake for Christmas.* She took a couple sleeping pills and went to bed.

Hours later, Dorine awoke to a frantic banging on the door. "HONEY! Op'n up. Fo'got m'key!" yelled a slurred, voice. She dragged herself out of bed, glancing at the clock that read 2 AM, and opened the door. Pete stumbled in. Standing in the middle of the living room, he swayed like a tree in the wind. All at once, "Gr-ra-ualp" and a volcano erupted all over the carpet. Then the "tree" lost his balance and fell into the vomit. At first, Dorine, didn't know whether to laugh or cry at the ridiculous scene. Pete looked like he could go to sleep right there, but she figured she better try to clean him up.

Her emotions darted like laser lights, first a flash of one color, then another. A streak of compassion hit her with the thought that perhaps he really couldn't help it, that he was trapped by an evil bigger than both of them. Then flashes of anger drove compassion away. *Why can't he see that he needs help? that AA can help? that if only he would go to church, perhaps God would set him free? Doesn't he want help? Doesn't he love me enough to try to get well?*

After Dorine got Pete cleaned up and awake enough to crawl into bed, she began to work on the *carpet. What if he never quits? I can't stand this anymore. Maybe I should divorce him.* "Please, God, I need help! Help me deal with my own emotions and this confusion."

The next morning, Dorine called her old friend, Marlene, "I'm desperate. I can't cope with it anymore. It's not just the drinking, but he's smoking in the house, and I get asthma and can hardly breathe. One time, he dropped a lit cigarette after coming home drunk and started a fire. If I hadn't been awake, I hate to think of what would have happened!"

"Come to Al-Anon with me tonight," Marlene invited. "This is a support group for anyone who is affected by someone's drinking. It will help you get your thinking straight."

So Dorine began attending Al-Anon meetings two or three times a week. The fellowship with others who had the same problem encouraged her, and she learned several things: Her spouse's problem was not her fault. Her spouse's recovery was not her responsibility. She learned not to take the symptoms of alcoholism personally, and not to be an "enabler." She received phone numbers of people she could call when she needed to talk. This helped.

However, the depression continued. How can you call someone when you're sinking? When a black cloud is engulfing you? How can you decide who to call, much less what to say?

Meanwhile, Lisa and Jack moved back to town and rented a house a block away. Jack had a month to get his family settled before leaving for Honduras for a Naval assignment.

"What's the matter, Mom?" was Lisa's first question at the airport. "You look sick."

Dorine made some vague comment about being tired, "... insomnia, because of arthritis."

"Here, Gramma," said little Sylvia, reaching out her arms. "A hug will make you feel better." Dorine knelt down to receive the hug from this precious girl who had been sending her colorful pictures and 'letters' she had 'written.' Oh yes, it did feel good. The sweet, childish smell and soft feel of her hair on Dorine's cheek, the arms tight and comforting around her neck, almost broke through her defenses.

"Let's go," she said, looking away so they wouldn't see her wipe away the tears.

Sylvia spent many hours at Grandma and Grandpa's house while her parents got settled.

Dorine began to feel there was a reason to get up in the morning. Sylvia brightened her days. Once, while coloring, Sylvia told Dorine about a kindergarten friend whose parents had gotten a divorce. "And she cried and cried. And I told God to make that bad divorce go away!" The words hit Dorine like a two-by-four. *Divorce is out of the question,* she decided. Later that day, she made an appointment to meet her Pastor for counseling.

Although this decision was made, the heavy cloud remained. *What is wrong with me? Why can't I be like others? I feel so worthless.* The counseling session opened up a small door of hope. The Pastor listened attentively and encouraged her. A few days later, as he had advised, she took Sylvia to a Christmas choir concert at the church.

Sylvia's eyes shone as she watched and listened and tapped her little hands on her lap in time to the music. The music grabbed Dorine's attention, also. After several songs, the choir began to sing, "O Little Town of Bethlehem." As she heard the familiar carol, Dorine suddenly had a new thought. *They are singing about me!* Grabbing a pen, she hurriedly scribbled on the bulletin:

I am Bethlehem --- little, insignificant, inadequate. How long have I lain here still, hoping for a glimmer of your glory, going through the motions day after day? As Dorine listened, jotting down ideas, she began to feel special, as if God had singled her out for a purpose. "Be born in me tonight," the choir sang. Her heart responded, *Yes, there is room in me for you. Shine in my dark streets and drive out the gloom. Give life and light to all in my world.* Dorine allowed the tears to flow freely in the darkness during the last song, as she talked to God in her heart. "Come into my heart, Lord Jesus. Forgive my sins. My life is yours. Take control of my emotions and fulfill your purpose in me."

Feeling an impulsive hug and kiss from Sylvia, Dorine smiled at her, returning the hug and wiping her tears. Her heart sang as they left the church.

On the way home, she listened to the happy chatter of her granddaughter while her thoughts organized into a speech for her husband. She would tell him she loved him, but that the alcoholic behavior must end. She would ask him to go with her to her next counseling session.

"Look Gramma!" Sylvia exclaimed, pointing to her Grandpa's truck. "I prayed Grampa would be home!"

This is different! A Saturday night and he's home early? Dorine parked, with a quick prayer for guidance.

They opened the door to see a sober man with red eyes. "I don't know what came over me," he said, "but when I went to the tavern, it seemed like the stupidest thing, and I couldn't go in. The very thought of drinking nauseated me. It seemed like I could see into my heart, and it looked black. I've been praying to God to forgive me." He began weeping again and put his arms around Dorine. "Please, will you forgive me, too? I want us to be a family again."

Dorine took a deep breath. "Are you willing to go to counseling with me about your alcoholism?"

"Yes." He nodded and looked sincerely into her eyes.

Dorine hugged and kissed her husband. "Yes, I forgive you. But I'll hold you to that as a promise."

Pete knelt down and hugged little Sylvia who said, "Jesus told me to tell you he loves you, Grandpa."

In the next few days, Dorine prepared for Christmas with a renewed interest. Lisa, Jack and Sylvia came over, and Kirk came home from college. They were all together for Christmas Eve dinner. As Pete read the chosen scriptures to them, Dorine's heart rejoiced. "The light shines in the darkness, and the darkness has not overcome it." (John 1:5). Jesus Christ, the Word become flesh, had driven out her darkness.

Chapter Nine

Deliver Me

Mara shifted in her pew after Pastor Jordan read, "I would not have known covetousness unless the law had said, 'You shall not covet'" (Romans 7:7b, NKJV).

Covetousness? Have I been coveting? Mara glanced at Scotty and Fran Doversham in the front pew. He was a wonderful man. She had only the highest respect for him.

Mara thought back about her husband's reaction when she'd exclaimed, "The best guitarist in the whole world will accompany me at the fair!"

"Good," Ben had said. "I hope you have fun."

Mara felt a stab of guilt. "You could come and listen," she ventured.

Ben shrugged. "Rick and I are going fishing."

Suddenly the sun dimmed. *Of course! Fishing is much more important than me! And so is hunting, and playing pool.*

Now, sitting alone in church, Mara wondered, "Is fishing more important to Ben than worshiping God?" If only she and Ben were united in their beliefs. She wished he were like Scotty. *He isn't just the best guitarist. He's the best man I've ever known!*

Mara glanced around. Did anyone suspect she hid a secret love? *Coveting is wrong. And God knows.*

Mara blinked back stinging tears. *I want to be in the same room with him. I draw strength from his vibrancy while listening to him teach or sing or play guitar. That can't be wrong, can it? Scotty seems to understand my deepest longings. When he called me a poet, I soared the rest of the day. When he told our Bible Study Group, "I need you in my life," I felt valued. Almost everything he says strikes a chord in me that whispers, "Here is your kindred spirit."*

Mara peeked again at Scotty. *Did he suspect how she felt? Did Fran? I wish I had a marriage like theirs. Yes, it is covetousness. But God, how do I deal with these feelings?*

All the next week, Mara wondered what to do. Her prayers seemed weak and unfocused. *Oh wretched woman that I am! Who will deliver me...?*

The following Sunday, as Scotty rose to sing Special Music, Mara's heart leaped. *How handsome he is!* The soothing song was one they had practiced together. She thought how his brown eyes flashed as he led Bible Studies. "We must learn to pray! We must believe God loves us, and care about each other." Surely the Holy Spirit had anointed him.

Scotty sat down, putting his arm around his wife, Fran. Mara, three pews back, twisted her wedding ring. *Why can't I have a husband like Scotty?* She closed her eyes against the turmoil raging inside. She must not let anyone know, or a scandal would surely follow, damaging her reputation and ministry, hurting this wonderful man of God. *What can I do, Lord?* she prayed. *I can't leave this church. I can't bear the thought of never seeing Scotty, but how can I keep love from showing in my eyes?* The inner argument continued. *It isn't wrong to love a Christian Brother if it is nonsexual, is it? But is it wrong to want intimate conversations? Brotherly hugs?*

Mara left church quickly. At home, she sank to her knees. *"Lord, please forgive me for covetousness. Cleanse me of this unrighteousness."* She sobbed. *"Lord, you know how hard it is. My husband seems to put so many other things ahead of you and me."*

Out in the kitchen, the screen door opened. *"Ben?"*

"Hi, Babe," Ben said cheerfully. "Bob and I are going to the pool tournament tonight. We'll get a motel and come home tomorrow night."

Tears came to Mara's eyes again. "You said we could spend some time together this evening."

"I'm sorry, Babe, but this is important to Bob."

"It's also important to spend quality time with your wife! We hardly ever do things together. I feel like second fiddle."

Ben's green eyes hardened as his cheerful mood evaporated. "You're so busy yourself that you don't have time for me either." He threw some clothes into a duffle bag and grabbed his toothbrush. "We'll talk later. Bye." He tried to plant a quick kiss on her cheek but she pulled away. He left quickly.

Mara flung herself on her bed. Tears of rage poured out. She choked out a prayer. *"Help, Lord; take over my emotions."* An ugly root of bitterness fought for attention. *"Lord, forgive me for resenting Ben's activities. He works hard, and needs time for recreation. But I'm so lonely! Also, I wish he felt the way I do about you. We don't have much in common."*

In the stillness, Mara sensed God speaking: *"I forgive you, but you must not continue coveting or resenting."*

"I know, Lord. Show me the way of escape."

An image came to Mara's mind. She saw Ben's flushed face as he bragged about the attentions of a woman at work. "She's interested in my activities," he had said. It had hurt to think of another woman conversing with her husband, connecting in a way she'd not been able to do. Did Fran feel like that? Did Ben feel that way when she talked about Scotty?

Mara sobbed, "I'm sorry, Lord. Forgive me for not accepting Ben as he is. Show me how to befriend Fran, too."

"The best way to befriend anyone," God seemed to reply, *"Is to pray for them, to place them in my hands."*

Peace settled over Mara as she prayed, "LORD Jesus, be in charge of my life and marriage. I trust you to use everything for your good purposes. Bless Ben and meet his needs. Now, in the name of Jesus Christ and by his strength and power, I rebuke covetousness, jealousy, and resentment. LORD, protect the marriage of Fran and Scotty. Thank you for the example of their marriage and their influence. In Jesus' name, Amen."

The change came gradually over the next few weeks. When Mara invited Fran to lunch, Fran confided happily, "Scotty leads me in Bible Study and prayer. He loves me as Christ loves the Church." Mara turned the pang of jealousy over to the Lord. After the next Bible Study, she helped Fran with lunch rather than talking with Scotty.

At home, Mara concentrated more on listening to her husband's heart.

"The sermons are way over my head," Ben said. "And I'll never know the Bible as well as Scotty. But sometimes, when I'm fishing, I feel God all around me."

When Ben left for his own activities without inviting her along, Mara kissed him goodbye, saying, "Have fun, Honey." She took time every day for private Bible Study, conversations with God, and for music. "Tune me up, Lord. Help me live in harmony with you. Fix whatever is wrong, and play your beautiful music through me."

An insight came one Sunday as she worshiped. *Although I love Scotty as a Christian brother, it's actually Jesus in him that attracts me.* Her friendship with Fran grew faster after that hindrance was released. Also, she began to see good characteristics in Ben that Scotty lacked, such as his down-to-earth way of describing situations.

One Saturday, Ben mentioned, "Maybe I'll go with you to that Bible Study tomorrow."

Mara smiled. "You'd do that for me?"

"Yes, but also for myself. I want to understand more. Maybe this is a good place to start."

At the Bible Study, Ben surprised Mara by his insights. Mara realized God must have brought her and Ben together for a reason and would use their difficulties for good.

She rejoiced to know that the sin of covetousness and its effects had been washed away.

God had delivered her.

Chapter Ten

Out of the Cage

Viola busied herself in the kitchen, fixing a fried chicken dinner, complete with a homemade jelly roll for dessert. A first anniversary deserved a special celebration, didn't it? Surely Manny would come home in time for supper this time.

Three hours later, the delicious aroma still hovered in the kitchen. Dejected, Viola took Manny's plate out of the 'hold warm' microwave and put it in the refrigerator. As she cleared the table, tears slid down her cheeks. *Couldn't he even call? I guess it's no special day to him.*

Viola sat back down at the table and tried to study her Bible lesson for Sunday, but questions plagued her. This wasn't the first time in their year of togetherness that Manny had been late. In fact, it happened more often lately. During the first four months, she'd told herself *it will get better. He just needs to feel more secure.* But it hadn't gotten any better.

Why is he like this? How can I cope with it? Who can I go to for help? Please, Lord, will you tell me how to live? Her tears poured out as she prayed.

Manny had convinced her when they met that he was recovering from alcoholism. His questions about Christianity made her feel needed. Certain that God could work through her love to save him, Viola ignored the danger signals in their relationship. Manny insisted they live together while waiting for his divorce to be final. Although this went against her religious training and convictions, she gave in when he threatened suicide. She had thought love and marriage would turn the wrong into right, that God would honor her efforts to help him get sober, to teach him about God's love. But after the simple wedding in their living room, not much changed. Manny still partied. She still felt guilty and confused.

What's the matter, God? Why won't you answer my prayers? Why won't you change him? Only the silence kept Viola company as she cried herself into an exhausted sleep.

The slam of Manny's truck door awakened Viola at 2 am. Her body stiffened as she heard him stagger to the door and fumble with the key. Fear clutched at her throat. *Drunk again! What should I do?...hide or wait quietly?*

Crash! She heard the lamp fall, then heard him swear. As his boots clumped toward the bedroom, Viola prayed again. *Help me, Lord Jesus, please help me!* She turned toward the wall, as far over as she could, and lay stll.

The bed shook as Manny dropped onto it. After a long minute, he reached for her and said in a slurred voice, "Hi Honey, how's my Babe?" He pulled her over and kissed her long on the mouth. Viola cringed with fear and disgust, nauseous at the smell of beer and marijuana. She tried to pull away, but he forced her back and kissed her again. Then he fell into a stertorous stupor.

The next day, Manny slept late as usual. "I thought you were starting that new job today," Viola said to him after he awoke.

"Have to get the truck fixed first. Alternator is going out. Gimme a check so I can fix it.

"I can't keep giving you money. We have to pay our rent."

"How can I work without my truck? Wanna let me use your car?"

"Last time you used my car," Viola reminded him, "you didn't get home until two in the morning and left the car out on the highway out of gas."

"OK. You use <u>your</u> car to go to work and I'll just stay here."

With a sigh, she gave him the checkbook. *No sense arguing. We're one in marriage, so I guess my money is ours and his is ours. I just wish he'd bring some of his home for bills.* Viola left for work after fixing Manny's oatmeal.

One evening, encouraged by a friend, Viola went to Al-Anon. "We can't change others, but we can change how we react to them," one woman said. When Viola mentioned seven bounced checks in the past month, another told her, "You don't have to be an enabler." Viola determined not to give in to Manny the next time.

He was still gone when she arrived home from the meeting. She read in the *One Day At a Time* book about enabling. It got her mind off worrying about him, and she went to sleep without even crying.

Crash! Bang! Slam! Viola looked at the clock. *Two a.m. again. This time I won't be intimidated.* Manny staggered to bed, stopping at the bathroom on the way to throw up. She gagged, listening.

"Hi, Honey," he said with a slurred voice. "I need some cig'rettes. Go get me some cig'rettes?"

Viola couldn't believe her ears. *At two am I should go to the store and get cigarettes?*

She pretended to be sleeping, but he pulled her over and said loudly, "Honey, I jus' need some cig'rettes. My truck is out of gas so I can't get any. Please?"

Remembering the Al-Anon meeting and what she had read, Viola decided not to give in to this whim. "No," she said quietly but firmly. This brought another louder explanation.

Viola said "No" again.

Suddenly Manny's hands were around Viola's neck, squeezing hard. She gasped and struggled to breathe. She managed to loosen his hands a little and said, "If you kill me, I'll go home to heaven, but you will have murder on your conscience the rest of your life." At that he squeezed harder, but soon let go and dropped over in a stupor.

Trembling, Viola listened to his snoring until convinced he was asleep for the night. She felt too shaky and sore to move for awhile.

Oh God! How did I get into such a mess?

After a few minutes, Viola got up and found an ice bag to put on her neck. At the table, she opened her Bible to Psalms, looking for one to match her emotions of fear, anger, confusion, frustration. The writer of Psalms seemed to have plenty of problems. But he also seemed to have found the secret...

Her eyes hurt too much to read. She folded her arms on the table, laid her head on them and cried until her chest ached. She blew her nose, then laid her aching head down again.

After a time, it seemed she could hear a voice in the silence. Not an audible voice, yet real. *How did you get into this mess?...by disobedience,* the voice seemed to whisper. *Your disobedience opened the door.*

Viola stayed still several minutes. She knew the voice was right. She had no excuse, for she knew the commandments. She'd known adultery was wrong. Marriage to Manny couldn't undo the previous wrong. Suddenly, all her rationalizing melted away into nothingness. This time when she wept, it was not self-pity or frustrated anger. She saw the blackness of her own disobedient heart and sensed the grief of a loving God.

Father, I'm sorry, really I am, she cried out in genuine repentance. *Please forgive me.* Opening her Bible, she read for a long time starting with 1 John 1:9. *O Lord Jesus, please take control of me, deep within me and throughout my life.* Then she fell asleep.

Manny seemed to be sorry the next day, when Viola showed him the marks on her neck. He agreed to allow a couple from church to come over to counsel them every week. Viola forgave Manny, hoping the incident had shocked him into sobriety. And he did stay sober for six weeks, longer than ever before. Or so she thought.

She soon learned he'd been smoking pot again. Soon he was back to his old partying habits, coming home at two am. Over the next few months, their relationship went from bad to worse, until one night she cried into the darkness, *Jesus, do you want me to hurt like this?* Suddenly, Viola sensed a benevolent presence. It seemed as if Jesus sat beside the bed, facing her and weeping as if his heart was broken, "No! No, I don't want you to hurt. I love you," he seemed to say.

Viola's mind quieted, and she remembered Jesus had paid the price for her freedom from sin and its power. It felt like she'd been trapped in a cage, but Jesus had opened the door and sat waiting for her to come out.

The next day, Viola called a Christian Psychiatrist which her pastor had recommended and made an appointment. After talking awhile and learning how Manny often treated Viola, he said he saw a picture in his mind of Manny coming after her with a knife. He advised her to separate from Manny for her physical safety. With help from friends, she changed the locks on her doors and sent Manny's clothes to a place he could pick them up. Then she filed for a restraining order.

With financial help from her church, Viola continued meeting with the Christian Psychiatrist until he pronounced her well, both spiritually and emotionally. She had learned that, by relying on Jesus and his saving grace, she could live in freedom. She praised God for opening the door and leading her out of the cage.

Chapter Eleven

For Better or Worse

My job at the University Hospital, the summer of my self-imposed separation from my second husband, seemed a Godsend. Working as a rehabilitation nurse helped me feel useful and skillful as I helped patients deal with paralyses or amputations, and resultant grief. This helped me avoid dwelling on my own problems. When I pinned "Kendra North, RN" onto my uniform, I no longer felt vulnerable to painful emotions.

I especially remember Kyle.

Kyle had been working with a steam shovel when suddenly the shovel wouldn't lift. He got down to fix it. After he'd replaced a loose bolt, the machine began rolling, knocking Kyle to the ground. He fell between the wheels, so wasn't crushed, but the blow to his back left him a quadriplegic. He came to rehab after a few weeks in the hospital.

"How do you feel, Kyle?" I asked one night, settling down to feed him.

"I'd be better off dead!" he muttered. "I'll never be able to work again."

Helplessness swept over me. I understood his feeling, since work was the only thing that made me feel worthwhile. Not knowing what to say, I silently fed him, keeping my thoughts to myself, wishing I could make him more comfortable.

My first marriage had failed and I'd almost given up on my second. My present husband's alcoholism convinced me he didn't love me. The stigma of divorce, and then of association with a practicing alcoholic had isolated me from friends. I was tired of Gene's excuses, of never knowing when he'd come home, of worrying that he might have an accident or lose his job, so I'd separated from him. But then I felt angry at myself for missing him and longing to see him.

Looking down at Kyle, helpless as a baby, I wondered what I'd do if I couldn't work. Oh, the blessed distraction of work.

We silently finished the meal. As days went by, I watched Kyle's relatives who visited him. They let him know they loved him, that he was worthwhile in spite of his helplessness. A gentle touch while telling him a funny story, showing him pictures his children had made for him, asking his opinion on certain issues all showed love.

The attitude of Kyle's wife especially impressed me. We developed a deep friendship over coffee breaks and lunches. She'd talk about practical changes now needed because of the quadriplegia, asking for advice about how to help him. But I never noticed a shadow of doubt in her that they'd cope with every problem together.

"God will give us strength to cope," she said.

Sometimes I thought Kyle accepted his condition extremely well. I wished I could do as well with my separation. But one night I walked in to find him sobbing bitterly. I patted his shoulder helplessly and prayed for guidance.

"Do you want to talk?" I asked. He continued convulsing with sobs, but didn't seem to indicate 'no,' so I pulled up a chair and waited. After he regained control, he lay quietly in the semi-darkness for a few moments. I wiped his eyes and helped him blow his nose.

"The worst thing about this is," he finally said, choking back another sob, "I'll have to divorce my wife. It's not fair to her to have to take care of me."

I leaned forward and brushed the hair away from his eyes. "Kyle, I've talked with your wife a lot these past weeks, and I know she loves you deeply. The accident hasn't dampened her love for you at all."

"I know, but she needs someone who can support her, someone she can look up to and have fun with," he replied.

A wish swept over me that I could have that type of husband. Then I felt guided to say, "When Karyn married you, didn't she promise to live faithfully with you in sickness or health, for better or worse?"

"Yes," he agreed.

"If you divorce her, she would feel like half her own being was cut off because you two are united. The "two became one.""

Kyle listened hungrily, as if he wanted to believe this.

"I know she wants you two to cope with every problem together," I continued. "As for support, I can vouch that, for a woman, love is the most important kind of support. The kind of love you have for her makes her feel precious and worthwhile and womanly. She looks up to you for your qualities of character, and you haven't lost those. Besides, two people in love can have fun together just being together."

Kyle's keen eyes seemed to see something I didn't. "Is that what you and your husband do?" he asked, "cope with every problem together?"

I blushed in the semi-darkness as I realized my "words of wisdom" were for me, also. We both quietly contemplated what I'd said until another patient's signal light beckoned me away.

As daylight streamed in the windows, I saw Kyle's wife arrive and found an excuse to pass his door. I saw a soft look in his eyes and a smile light up his face when he saw her. The depression and tension he'd had seemed to be gone.

Finishing my shift that morning, I felt I needed to make an important decision. My words rang in my ears: "Two became one…in sickness and health, for better or for worse…." I knew the disease of alcoholism had told me a lie. My husband did love me, but had agreed to the separation because he felt it wasn't fair for me to have to put up with his disease. Feeling powerless, he had recently begun to attend AA meetings.

After sleeping a few hours that day, I sat down at my desk and wrote a note to my husband: "Dear Gene, I love you. I'm willing to end the separation if you want to. No bargains or conditions; I just want to be your wife. Love, Kendra."

He did want to. He proudly introduced me to his friends in AA. We began reading together out of the blue book and the Bible and praying together. It wasn't easy, but as we coped with every problem together, we gained a new honesty and intimacy in our marriage.

That was five years ago. Kyle learned at the rehab center how to cope with quadriplegia. He and Karyn have a happy life together. Recently Gene received his "five years of sobriety" medal. He says he couldn't have done it if I hadn't stuck by him "for better or worse."

Personal Experience Stories

Chapter Twelve

A Glimpse of God's Love

"Babe, we just need to let her go. It won't help to agonize about it," Martin said. He gently squeezed my hand. I marveled at his calmness, knowing his heart must ache about his teenage daughter, who had run away the day before, three weeks after our wedding.

"I'm not blaming you, Babe" he continued. "We can't protect her if she insists on her own way."

Although he agreed with my discipline, I felt I'd failed. I also felt cheated because I hadn't had enough time to win her over. My thoughts went back and forth. *How could I have handled it differently? I should have...what?*

I couldn't answer that question.

Neither could I figure out how I could have lived the earlier part of my life differently. A few years earlier, when my husband of 17 years divorced me, I felt love-starved and vulnerable. Losing my trust that God loved me, because he didn't answer my prayers the way I wanted, led to an oppressive confusion. Because I was spiritually and emotionally sick, I'd fallen into an adulterous relationship with a drug addict/alcoholic, whom I thought I could 'save.' Because of that, my kids wouldn't stay with me, either. My life was a mess.

Then, God did a work of spiritual and emotional healing in me through Christian counseling and a loving, supportive church group. As they prayed scripture over me, God spoke to my heart with comfort and reassurance. Feeling like God had rescued me from a "pit," I'd regained my trust in His love.

Yet, the current incident with my stepdaughter opened old wounds and fears of inadequacy and failure. It unleashed a storm of conflicting feelings in me with accompanying negative self-talk: *"... married only three weeks and already I've failed. Whatever made me think God meant Joel 2:25 for me—that he would restore anything in my life? What makes me think I deserve anybody's love?*

The fact that my two boys seemed happy to continue visiting us, since the wedding, comforted me some. We went to our friends' home and tried to enjoy the 4th of July party. Sitting on blankets in the back yard, we ate grilled hamburgers and salads. "Look at those dark clouds!" someone exclaimed. "Sure hope the fireworks display won't be canceled." As we visited outwardly, on the inside I kept talking to Jesus.

Lord, it hurts! It's not just that I'm worried about her. I'm also worried about me. Am I a hopeless failure? Will my life ever be right? Have I displeased you so much that you won't work in my life anymore? Am I deceiving myself again?

After the heartbreak of divorce and then of three years "in the pit," I'd been afraid to love again, to trust again. Yet, while considering remarriage, God reassured me with a "vision." I saw Jesus, Martin, and I dancing around in a circle, laughing. A child joined our circle, then two more, then others, then it was back to the three of us again. Jesus looked happy. This had given me the courage to marry again.

But now, the day after Martin's daughter left, we didn't feel like dancing. *Lord, you promised to guide me continually. Have I made a mistake in the way I talked to her?*

After eating, Martin and I settled on blankets on the grassy slope above the lake to wait for darkness and the fireworks display. A few sprinkles of rain came down now and then, but not enough to drive us inside. We watched the kids enjoy themselves. "Hey, look at that smoke bomb! Here, let's light this Piccolo Pete."

Suddenly, at dusk, we heard a gasp. "Look! A rainbow above the lake." There we saw the most brilliant rainbow I'd ever seen. "There's two --- a double rainbow!" someone shouted. I jumped up to get a better look. How beautiful it was! And this rainbow was genuine. All at once, it seemed like God's Spirit spoke in my heart about another rainbow—the promise to Noah. I remembered the scripture in Isaiah 54:9&10:

"For this is like the days of Noah to me: as I swore that the waters of Noah should no more go over the earth, so I have sworn that I will not be angry with you and will not rebuke you. For the mountains may depart and the hills be removed, but my steadfast love shall not depart from you, and my covenant of peace shall not be removed, says the Lord, who has compassion on you," (RSV).

I gazed at the double rainbow in awe. It seemed God was telling me, "It's not your fault your step-daughter ran away. You didn't make a mistake in marrying Martin. You are now living in my will. My love will strengthen you and be with you whatever comes. You are doubly forgiven. And as long as you follow my guidance, you will have peace."

My heart swelled with praise: *Oh, thank you, Lord! Thank You that in Your love You are guiding me and will continue to guide me!*

My husband came alongside and put his arm around me. "Do you like the rainbow, Babe?" I turned to him with a smile and quoted the verses to him. "You see?" he said. "God's not mad at you."

Four years passed before she came back to us but now, 30 years later, I see a beautiful transformation in my step-daughter. I look back on the 17-year marriage with her dad and see how God patiently healed us and refined us. He helped us through many trials and problems, including the ten-month bout with cancer that took Martin's physical life but left us both with reassurance of his eternal life.

Today I can truly say God has restored to me what the 'locusts' have eaten. (Joel 2:25). That's grace—undeserved mercy!

Chapter Thirteen

Battle with Cancer

"Thank goodness Judy's here. Now everything will be all right."

Surprised at the words from my dad, I smiled and greeted family members grouped around his bed. During the 1600 mile journey from Washington to Minnesota, I had slept and prayed alternately while my husband drove steadily for 24 hours. Feeling inadequate, I wondered what my dad thought I could do to help. Lung cancer had metastasized to his bones and then to his brain. The doctor had sent him to the nursing home to die. *Lord, how should I pray for him? Please, use me as your instrument.*

My mother looked exhausted from many weeks of helping to care for him. I felt I could at least help her by staying with him so she could go home and rest. Cancer had demented his brain but I thought I knew, after many years of working in nursing homes, how to deal with demented patients. It seemed God had given me a gift for calming and comforting them. Perhaps my being here with Dad would help them both sleep more peacefully.

"I'll stay with him through the night. You all go home and get some sleep."

My sisters and Mom helped Dad into a wheelchair before they left, and I wheeled him to the door to say goodbye. That was my first mistake. He grabbed the door frame and wheeled himself outside and over to the car. Although the cancer made it impossible for him to walk, his arms were strong and we all had difficulty loosening his grip from the car door. My mother was afraid he would pull himself to a standing position which would shatter the cancer-riddled bones, leaving him in a heap on the ground. Finally, an orderly helped us get him back inside, and they left for her house.

The next few hours with him were exhausting. I prayed silently, *Lord, give me strength and wisdom. How do I humor him to keep him from getting more upset without him getting into trouble?* A nurse walked by and smiled at me. Knowing from my previous work as a nurse how busy they must be, I assumed she was glad I was there to watch him so they could spend more time with other patients.

Continuing to pray silently, I stayed with Dad as he wheeled himself all over the facility like a caged animal looking for a way out. Attempts at rational conversation didn't work. He grabbed a telephone and dialed 911. I reached behind him and pressed down the button to hang up as he began to tell someone he was imprisoned and "they" were trying to murder him so someone should come right away. (Later, I found out he had actually gotten through to 911 three times.) I tried to talk to him, to convince him that no one was trying to hurt him—that it was the cancer, not the people. At first he had acted like he believed I was on his side, but after more tries with the telephone, he realized I had prevented the connections. Anger radiated from him like heat from a boiler ready to blow up. *Lord, how do I help him? What should I do? He seems so tormented!"*

After what seemed like several hours (but may have been only a couple), he wheeled himself back to his room and headed for the bathroom. I helped him transfer to the stool, but in the process he grabbed my arm and squeezed tightly with his fingernails digging in until the blood ran. His eyes shot daggers of hatred as he swore at me. I burst into tears. "Daddy, let go! You're hurting me! I can't help it you're sick; you don't have to take it out on me!"

When he didn't let go, I heard myself blurt out, "In the name of Jesus Christ, I command you evil spirits to quit tormenting my Dad! Get out of here!" His fingers relaxed. The fight left him and he let go of my arm. I couldn't quit crying for a few minutes, since my pent-up emotions needed release.

When I noticed a flicker of recognition in his eyes, I said through my tears, "Daddy, I love you. I'm sorry you have cancer." He meekly allowed me to help him back to the wheelchair. Orderlies came to help him to bed. When he was settled for sleep and they had gone, Dad said in a heart-wrenching voice, "They're trying to take my soul away!"

My heart went out to him. *Please, Holy Spirit, guide me what to say, what to do. Please give him your peace.* I knew he had become a Christian when I was a child. He had made sure we all went regularly to church, Sunday School, Bible Camp, Confirmation Class and Luther League. Yet, I was unsure whether he had given up his faith in recent years. Believing God had sent me there for a purpose, I took courage.

Holding his hand, wondering how lucid he was, I said, "No, Daddy, they can't take your soul away. Remember? Jesus promised no one can snatch us out of his hand. If we believe in him, we will go to Heaven when we die." Daddy closed his eyes, took a deep breath, and gently squeezed my hand, as if receiving what I said.

"Daddy, remember the Apostles' Creed? Will you recite it with me?" His eyes stayed closed and I wasn't sure if he was ignoring me or had fallen asleep.

I felt it was important that he confess his faith, for the Bible says, "If you confess with your lips that Jesus is Lord and believe in your heart that God raised him from the dead, you will be saved," (Rom. 10:9 RSV). I patted his shoulder and asked again.

"Do you still believe, Daddy? Please recite it with me: "I believe in God the Father Almighty, maker of heaven and earth ---" I waited a moment, then rejoiced to hear him saying the words. I repeated them with him, and we went on to recite the rest together: "... and in Jesus Christ his only Son our Lord, who was conceived by the Holy Ghost, born of the virgin Mary, suffered under Pontius Pilate, was crucified, dead, and buried. He descended into hell; the third day he rose again from the dead; he ascended into heaven, and sits on the right hand of God the Father Almighty; from thence he shall come to judge the quick and the dead. I believe in the Holy Ghost, the holy Christian church, the communion of Saints, the forgiveness of sins, the resurrection of the body, and the life everlasting. Amen."

Daddy's voice was weak, but clear as he recited the whole creed with me. After we also prayed the Lord's Prayer together, he fell asleep. It felt like Spiritual Darkness had fled in defeat. I hoped his torment would not return.

By the time my mother arrived in the morning to relieve me of my vigil, I was too exhausted to say much other than, "He had a rough time for a while, but has been sleeping peacefully the last few hours." I went to their house and slept, but had nightmares of demons.

It was late afternoon by the time Mom came back home and gave me a report. "It was the first time I've seen him really lucid for weeks!" She smiled gently, looking down. "He told me he loves me." Her face looked much more relaxed than the day before as she related more of their conversation. I silently praised the Lord for his grace and smiled at her. "And then he said, "forget the bad, remember the good." Later, the Pastor came by and we had communion together. Frank even prayed the Lord's Prayer with us --- every word! Now he's sleeping peacefully."

My spirit rejoiced as I prayed silently, *Thank you, Lord, for using me as your instrument and for giving my dad peace.*

After Mom and I had supper together, I went back to the nursing home to stay with my dad again. He seemed peaceful, without a sign of the torment of the night before, but terribly weak. I fed him a little jello. The doctor came in and told me what to expect --- that the cancer would draw Dad further and further into a coma until he slipped away.

It was a quiet night. I sang songs to him, quoted scripture, talked to him, and prayed. He tried to talk once; it sounded like "I love you." I wasn't sure most of the time if he was sleeping or comatose. The next two nights, he didn't even try to talk or move.

Sunday morning (Mother's Day, 1992), I ached all over when I went to Mom's to sleep. *I must have the flu. Spiritual battle sure takes a toll on a person.* Nightmares continued when I did drop off to sleep. A few hours later, Mom returned with the news: Dad was gone. Suddenly, I felt a joyful peace in my soul. *The battle with cancer is over and his soul was not taken away!* I felt like singing the song by Bill & Gloria Gaither that says, "It is finished! The battle is over! It is finished. There'll be no more war. It is finished, the end of the conflict. It is finished, and Jesus is Lord!"

Chapter Fourteen

I Am Bethlehem

We expect Christmas to be a joyous time. But for many, Christmas simply intensifies feelings of hopelessness and loneliness.

Many years ago, I struggled with depression as Christmas drew near. Wanting to keep my commitment as a choir member, I forced myself to participate in the Christmas concert. I broke down in tears before we entered the sanctuary. Friends, knowing my situation, hugged me. They gave me strength to compose myself and prepare to sing. As the concert proceeded, I began to listen with my heart to the words we sang:

"O little town of Bethlehem, how still we see thee lie. Above thy deep and dreamless sleep the silent stars go by; yet in thy dark streets shineth the everlasting light. The hopes and fears of all the years are met in thee tonight."

Dark streets. That sounds gloomy. That sounds like me.

As we went on to the second and third verses, I began to see what God was doing behind the scenes. "Where meek souls will receive Him still, the dear Christ enters in."

Suddenly, I sensed that God was speaking to me through the words of the song.

I am Bethlehem!

I thought of the verse in Galatians 4:4, "But when the time had fully come, God sent forth his Son, born of woman, born under the law, to redeem those who were under the law, so that we might receive adoption as sons. And because you are sons, God has sent the Spirit of his Son into our hearts crying, "Abba! Father!" (Gal. 4:4-6, RSV).

Between songs, I quickly jotted down my thoughts on my bulletin. By the time the concert was over, I felt more hopeful and less lonely than I had in a long time. God's truth and presence were lighting up my darkness. This poem resulted from that experience.

I am Bethlehem... little, insignificant, inadequate in my eyes.
How long have I lain here still, hoping for a glimmer of Your glory,
going through the motions day after day?
LORD, You gave a promise through prophets long ago.
Will Your promise be fulfilled in me?
Will my purpose be fulfilled?
Above me, the stars are silent. My heart aches with their silence.
I anguish to hear Your voice.
But suddenly! Has the time fully come?
Here You are, shining in the dark streets of my heart, driving out gloom.
In Your radiance, You speak, giving Your Word flesh!
Therein my hopes are fulfilled, my fears dispelled.
O Glorious LORD! There is room in me for You!
Fill me to overflowing with Your glory!
Shine and speak through me.
Make Your music resound through me that others may know the song You've given,
the peace You have brought.
Is this my purpose?...that You have come to be born in me?

This reminder by the Holy Spirit, that Jesus did indeed come to earth to be "born in me" (i.e. received by me as Savior and LORD) made my troubles fade into insignificance.

Like Bethlehem of old, the only significance I need is to be a dwelling place of Christ. He is Emmanuel, God with us in all our problems. He gives us significance, adequacy, hope and comfort. He makes my heart want to sing with the joy of His presence.

Chapter Fifteen

Two Angelic Rescues

"For he will give his angels charge of you to guard you in all your ways," Psalm 91:11.

"Because he cleaves to me in love, I will deliver him; I will protect him because he knows my name.

"When he calls to me I will answer him; I will be with him in trouble, I will rescue him and honor him. With long life I will satisfy him and show him my salvation," (Psalm 91:14-16).

"Seeing is believing" is a phrase people often use. But sometimes it is more true that "believing is seeing."

On a snowy day in Moses Lake, Washington, I wouldn't have driven on the icy roads if I didn't have to. However, my patient needed me to show up.

Patti's multiple sclerosis had progressed to the point that she was bed fast and unable to do any personal care. She was dependent on her husband and on me, a nurse. Her husband fed her breakfast and did the necessary morning care, then left to teach school. I usually arrived an hour or two later to turn her and bathe her, whatever she needed.

I drove slowly and carefully through the streets, aware of the ice. After I turned off the main road, my car suddenly jack-knifed and headed straight into a snowbank. With snow up to the windows, I could not get out of the car.

I put the car into reverse and gunned the motor. The car didn't budge. I tried to rock back and forth but that didn't help. I was stuck tight. This was before cell phones, so I couldn't call anyone. No one was in sight. I tried to open the car door, but the snow kept it shut tight.

"Dear Lord Jesus, what should I do? Please help me out of this snow bank."

I breathed deeply for a couple of minutes. All of a sudden I felt the car move! I looked out the windows and didn't see anybody. But it felt like someone lifted the car. Soon the car was out of the snowbank and on the street, facing the way I needed to go. I looked out the windows to see who I should thank, but I could not see anyone.

I thanked and praised God for sending angels to rescue me and drove to Patti's house.

****

Several years later, after Patti died, I had a different job. I was night charge nurse in a nursing home fifty miles away. In order to get to work on time, I had to leave Moses Lake by 10 pm. My shift lasted from 11 pm to 7 am, but I often had to work overtime so might not get home until 9:30 am or later. I usually could not sleep later than 1:30 pm.

The weather was near blizzard conditions that night. I felt tired and discouraged from not enough sleep. I called to see if I could get someone to take my place, but no one could. Someone had to care for the nursing home residents.

I started early so I could drive slowly. Near the turnoff to I-90, visibility was so bad I could not see the road. I turned where I thought I needed to, but soon realized I was in a big ditch or field. I felt disoriented, but prayed for guidance. Soon, I found the turnoff and drove onto the highway.

I crept along, straining to see ahead of me. Within a couple of miles, a truck came up behind. Knowing it would spray snow if it passed me, I began to panic. But I kept praying and concentrated on the white line at the side of the highway. The truck passed me. In the snowy spray I could see nothing! I felt the car go off the road and yelled, "Jesus! Get me back on the road." It was impossible to steer so I let go of the steering wheel.

Within a couple of minutes, my car was back on the highway. I slowed down even more to catch my breath. Thanking God profusely for sending his angels to protect me and help me, I calmed down and felt joy and peace.

During the rest of the trip, the snow lightened up enough so it wasn't so scary. I was able to drive a decent speed.

The next morning on my way home, the sky was clear. I looked at the place where I had gone off the road and saw posts at intervals. *How did I navigate between the posts without hitting them?*

The angels God sent to rescue me sure knew what they were doing.

Chapter Sixteen

Patches of Fog/Lasting Beauty

"Patches of fog won't hold up under sun."

I clipped this intriguing phrase out of a newspaper, pondering its meaning. "Patches of fog" reminded me of the confusion and depression I'd experienced. I had recently written this poem, expressing my feelings:

"Lord, give me clear sailing," is what I often cry

when I feel the fog's so thick I'd really rather die.

Then, just for a moment, He'll cause the fog to lift.

But He says, "My grace, sufficient, is the greater gift.

"When at last, you've stood the test," He gently lets me know,

"you'll receive the crown of life. The trials help you grow.

God didn't abandon me in the fog; He sent sunshine to penetrate it and break it up.

"Patches of fog won't hold up under sun" became a promise to me that eventually the depression and confusion would be gone. But like most promises, it is linked with responsibility. I had to choose whether or not to expose my "fog" to the sun. When I did, God revealed underlying attitudes of rebellion, self-righteousness and resentment. As I confessed these, (i.e. "laid them out in the sun"), He forgave me and cleansed me.

God sent His sunshine through other Christians, also. They prayed and talked with me—when I sought them out. I could feel His light and warmth driving away the fog as

I attended worship services, sang praises, prayed, read my Bible, and listened to Christian music. The sun couldn't shine on me if I hid in a cubby hole. I needed to get out into the sunshine to let it warm me and lighten my heart.

Some fog seemed endless. However, God works in fog as well as in light. The Psalmist mentions God riding on the clouds. Perhaps I needed to experience it in order to call out to God. When I called to Him in my distress, God delivered me and began to work out His loving purpose in me.

The Psalmist says, "The LORD does whatever pleases him, in the heavens and on the earth,.... He makes clouds rise from the ends of the earth; he sends lightning with the rain and brings out the wind from his storehouses," (Psalm 135:6-7, NIV).

These verses seemed to say to me, "When your world is coming to an end, God is the one who makes it foggy and scary and bitterly cold." Why would He do this? He must have a good reason. I came to realize I'd been clinging to some idols. Other people, my emotional needs, my natural desire to be loved and appreciated, had become more important to me than obedience to God. He knows it is best for us to worship Him alone. It took a storm to rip me away from idols to which I had clung.

Jesus came to me in my cloud of depression and confusion, warming my emotions with reassurances of love. This sunlight gradually broke my fog into patches and drove it away. Now, if I hit a patch of confusion or depression, I turn to God, exposing my heart to His sunlight through His Word, prayer, worship, or Christian fellowship. Soon the fog is gone.

"Patches of fog won't hold up under sun;" they disappear.

Lasting Beauty

The heavy fog that had settled over our town also gave me an object lesson. Combined with the right temperature, it formed beautiful hoarfrost on all the trees, fences, and telephone lines. I sensed God saying, "See, I not only drive away the fog, but I use it to create beauty in your life." He had worked in the midst of my confusion and depression, transforming it into good.

I wondered how long the hoarfrost would last. Often it lasts only a day or two in that part of the country (Moses Lake, WA). I asked God, "Is the beauty You have created in my life going to last?"

God continued my object lesson. The next day, I was dazzled by the beauty of my surroundings as the hoarfrost glittered in the sunshine. It didn't melt for several days, The beauty remained, although the fog was gone. This conveyed the message: *The beauty God created in you will last.*

God delights in transforming the evil Satan means against us into good. This is what Jesus came to do. He declared the fulfillment of scripture when he read from the prophet Isaiah's scroll. "The Spirit of the Lord is on me, because he has anointed me to preach good news to the poor. He has sent me to proclaim freedom for the prisoners and recovery of sight for the blind, to release the oppressed, to proclaim the year of the Lord's favor. (Luke 4:18-19, NIV).

God is faithful to His promises (Psalms 145:13). He can do a good work in you, too. The beauty He creates will last.

Chapter Seventeen

Charlie's Legacy

Life had been a struggle. After my husband died of cancer, I'd wandered in a "wilderness," searching for a purpose to validate my existence. I didn't care to remain on earth. My faith in God kept me keeping on, but I felt of little use to anyone at the age of 60. I felt lonely, empty, and insignificant.

Then I met Charlie.

Well, I didn't actually *meet* him. We became pen pals through the internet. Charlie and I shared the pain of losing a spouse and similar feelings about grief. He'd cared for a paraplegic wife for fifteen years until she'd died seven years earlier.

We shared a love for music: "the organ is limited only by the player's imagination." he wrote. "I use it as my worship to my Lord. I feel His presence take over and the music comes... maybe a hymn, but mostly the joy or sorrow on my soul ... for hours, then It leaves and I am back to plunk, plunk. I find it therapeutic ...."

We shared similar values, hopes and dreams. Charlie volunteered for Meals-On-Wheels and the cancer society. I volunteered music at nursing homes. We knew the joy of giving. "You cannot out give GOD..." he wrote.

We wrote our deep, inner feelings to each other. "I haven't been productive since my husband and Mom died. It feels like I'm drifting aimlessly. It's hard to concentrate. That restless, lonely feeling is why I signed up on the singles site two weeks ago."

Charlie understood my heart. His words gave me courage: "Take hope. The sun still shines and God is still there."

I answered: "Your letters bring sunshine into my life."

Through daily e-mails, we shared worries of his daughter's cancer scare, his dear housekeeper's death, and his diagnosis of right ventricular cardiomyopathy.

After six weeks of corresponding, I spent New Year's Eve wishing I could marry someone 3000 miles away, whose heart was about to quit beating. He'd given me the desire to live. I no longer felt lonely, depressed, or hopeless.

Because of his heart problem, Charlie was hesitant to get serious. He tried to hold his feelings back. "It is many years since I've had the feeling someone other than my children even knew I existed. I cherish the feeling and hate myself for being such a 'fraidy cat, fearful of putting a toe in the water of life. I ask the Lord for an answer and the only feeling I get is wait. I also have the feeling that you, my dear, are going to end up doing bigger and better things for the Kingdom. As for dropping things I do for the less fortunate, how can I? When our Lord said pick up your cross and follow me, he never said how heavy it would be."

As I read that, an idea landed with a thud in my heart. I wrote in my journal: "Has God chosen me to be Charlie's Simon of Cyrene? That's not encouraging. Simon carried the cross up the hill, then Jesus died on it. Does this mean I'm to help Charlie get ready to die?"

I'd hoped to do "bigger and better things," especially as a writer. But, *maybe my "bigger and better thing" is to encourage a man of quality character, deep love for Jesus Christ, and compassion for the down and out. Maybe my purpose is to convince him he is lovable and wonderful and can soar with joy as he serves the LORD with his life.*

The love and encouragement of a wonderful man could make the difference between a desert and a fruit-bearing garden. I'd believed God would choose someone special for me. I thought it might be Charlie.

After two months of correspondence, we expressed love for each other. "I am awed by your words... never felt the power of words as I do when they come from you. Never before have I known such deep love. If only, Judith ... I love you forever! Do your hands get tired lately? They may, because they are holding my heart."

Charlie's expressions of love and his daily emails healed a hurt deep inside me. He sent cherished mementos and gifts, so I felt pampered as never before. But the free and easy communication was the most special, because my words were accepted and appreciated.

We kept hoping for healing, even while his episodes of palpitations came more frequently. We believed Psalm 37:4, "Delight yourself in the Lord and he will give you the desires of your heart."

Charlie said, "If it is meant to be, it will be."

"Bless you, Charlie. Even if we can't be together physically, you've granted me my heart's desire... to have a soul-mate to feel in tune with like we belong together, our hearts beating together, one in spirit.

"God led us together for some good reason," I told him. "If you die, it will soften the grief to know I helped make your last months happy. You are like a valuable diamond, and I feel I've been chosen to bring out your luster so others can see it."

Charlie wrote: "Before you, I was alive but did not live. Before you, I smiled, but did not laugh. Before you, I didn't know how to love and hid behind a wall. … if my time here is to end before our wishes come true, I want you to know these last weeks have been the happiest days of my life. You've let me experience the wonder and joy of a shared Christian committed love that is granted with approval by God himself. I know no higher gift that can be given to a man than to be loved by what the Bible calls a virtuous woman. Judith, you are all I ever dreamed of and more. Thank you, my dear."

In his new confidence, Charlie decided to help an abused woman and her children by turning his house into a halfway house. "They look like refugees from Biafra." After a couple weeks, he wrote, "It is amazing to see the change.... They are blossoming. She thinks she may have a job, so she is ecstatic."

I began to see God's hand in our situation. Was his purpose for us to marry, or to heal us so we each could complete the work we'd been created to do? Charlie's joy and peace in providing a halfway house brought me joy and peace, also.

He talked of doing more with music. "I've never felt inspired to be or do anything before you. Now, I feel led to do all I can to expand the Savior's Kingdom. You've removed the fear of rejection from me. I know you'll never scoff but will encourage me. Maybe for a finale, we could have a thunderous piano/organ duet of The HOLY CITY." Genuine love helps loved ones grow and become what they were meant to be.

Charlie promised "if we are granted our wishes, I will give all I have, and pray for more, to give to you the best Christian husband you could wish for. But if not, if I have made you feel loved, cherished, and appreciated, that is reward enough for me."

We weren't granted our wishes for marriage. Charlie died in his recliner with a smile, holding a picture of me. Yet he made me feel cherished even after death. His daughter sent his goodbye letter. It said, "I've been the recipient of the purest love possible. I'd like to be remembered, but not grieved. I hope I've helped you realize you're a precious woman and such a rare find that you deserve nothing but the best. I'm nowhere near that, so maybe the Lord is getting you ready for the real one. You are too young and vital to wither away. So please,... keep your eyes open for the one that God has personally picked and chosen for you.

"Your pure, sweet nature and open demeanor with Christian love showing through you made me realize how small I was, and how wonderful a gift it is to have a woman like you openly say she loves you. You will still make some lucky man the most wonderful wife in the world. I wish it could have been me. Since it isn't, God is getting you ready for the real one."

In spite of his death and my grief, I believe God did "exceedingly abundantly above all I could ask or think," (Eph.3:20 KJV). Charlie's love gave me the motivation and strength I need to finish my work. I'd thought the reason we became acquainted was so I could minister to him, helping him carry his cross. But God knew I needed his love to complete my purpose for living. Even the grief was part of the plan. I had a sense of giant puzzle pieces fitting together.

Later, Charlie's daughter accepted the Lord. She wrote, "I heard Dad's voice saying it was my time now and not to waste it. I... felt a sense of going home. My heart is full of love for everyone." What a joy to learn Charlie's most fervent prayer had been answered! "Our whole family life has changed now as we are starting to realize the impact and legacy that one man has had...." Her nephew, and then her husband, also accepted the Lord. "The change in him is unbelievable! Christian love is so much deeper and better. I hope God sends you the mate you deserve to further your Christian walk."

They prepared Charlie's house for abused women and children, as he had requested. In the front entry, a brass plaque reads, "This facility is dedicated to the Glory of GOD in memory of our dad." Meanwhile, the first guests of the halfway house moved into an apartment and seemed to be happy and doing well with life.

It comforted me to hear all this. Grief is easier to bear if one can see a purpose in it. Months after his death, I wrote in my journal, "Thank you, Charlie, for being obedient to the Heavenly vision you saw. You obediently gave your money and home for missions and ministries. You gave your time to cheer up little old ladies, including me. You rescued a family from the pit of despair, and rescued me from—

"What was it you rescued me from, Charlie? Remember? I knew I should write but had lost the will, the motivation. Now I want to write all day long. You rescued me from the feeling of not mattering to anyone, just as you appreciated me for letting you know you mattered to me.

"Why did God bring us together, Charlie?... to help you get ready to die and to re-motivate me? A bigger purpose than either of us dreamed will unfold as time goes on. After the bad news end of December, we had two beautiful, love-filled months-- the most wonderful months of my life. I felt nurtured as never before and will never be the same, but healthier. God does work in everything for good."

Charlie revealed God's grace to me. He'd looked into the depths of my being and loved what he saw there. He had validated me (as the dictionary says, "made me no longer weak or defective, but sound and well-grounded." I vowed to serve the Lord – not as Charlie's wife as I'd hoped, but still as an instrument of God's grace.

Now, (I wrote in 2014) several years after the end of our three and a half months of correspondence, I am happily married to the "real one" for whom Charlie got me ready--- the soul-mate in spirit, soul, and body whom God intended. Because of Charlie and his validation, I dared get back on the internet and find another pen pal (Paul). Because of Charlie's validation, I could trust Paul. Because Charlie understood me, I could become an understanding wife to Paul who loves me like Christ does and like Charlie did. This was Charlie's legacy to me and to Paul.

(Paul and I were married for sixteen years before he died in 2022.)

Chapter Eighteen

Someone to Love

After several hours at the computer, I sighed. *"Lord, I want to write for you, but it's not working."* I let my hands drop off the keyboard and slumped back in my chair. *"I don't have the emotional energy to concentrate. It feels like I'm drifting aimlessly. Please, Lord,... help me?"*

For years I'd been convinced God had called me to write. I'd sold several manuscripts to Christian periodicals, but then my husband's cancer in 2003 disrupted everything. God sustained and comforted me during the ten months of Martin's cancer ordeal, and after his death, attending Grief-share meetings helped me deal with the grief of his death.

However now, two years later, I wasn't doing so well.

I shut down the computer, plodded to the dark living room, and looked out at the night sky. I'd been determined to remain a widow in order to have more time to concentrate on writing. *"But Lord, I'm so lonely. How can I write without someone to love, to love me, to give me the emotional energy and support to write? I feel dried up and empty, struggling with loneliness."* Sitting at the table, I rested my head in my hands.

Previously, through many difficult lessons of life, I'd learned to trust God enough so that, during Martin's cancer treatments, I could say to God through my tears, *"I know you are holy and righteous. My life is in your hands and you know what you are doing. Your will be done."* Scripture had given me hope. My relationship with God had given me peace and joy, even in the midst of pain.

I wiped my eyes and wondered, *so why do I feel such loneliness now, that seems to sap the motivation out of me?*

I got up for a drink of water, then returned to the window. As I gazed into the darkness, a Bible verse came to mind: "Take delight in the Lord, and he will give you the desires of your heart. Commit your way to the Lord; trust in him and he will act," (Psalm 37:4-5 RSV). It felt like God asked, "What is your desire? What would you like?"

Touched that he would ask, I prayed, "Lord, do you want me to stay single the rest of my life? I'm willing, if that's your will. But it sure would be nice to have a husband who loves you as much as I do, who loves me and is my soulmate. Either way, will you please take away this loneliness and give me the ability to concentrate on writing? More than anything, I want to fit into your plan for my life."

Over the next couple days, I felt an urge to look on the internet for a Christian singles' site. I asked God about this, afraid it could be a temptation from the devil, but it seemed like he gave me a go-ahead signal.

Wanting to correspond with a Christian, I filled out a profile saying I wanted a man "just like Jesus." That site replied I was unmatchable and rejected my profile. Later, I found a different site that had a good definition of Christian marriage and wonderful devotionals for singles. I filled out a profile and began searching for a pen pal, constantly praying for guidance.

At some point, I wrote this poem, expressing my longings:

Someone

Are you out there? The one who is in God's plan for me?

The one to whom I can talk for hours in a "friendship deep and clean?"

I want to tell you who I am—every corner and hidden closet.

I want to know who you are, past, present, future dreams and hopes.

If I can give you courage and a joy in living, and you can give me

strength and clarity, then we can soar together.

Where are you? Have I met you yet?

Or am I to live for Christ alone?

My first pen pal was Charlie from Canada. It was exciting to have someone to write to every day and we quickly became emotionally close. We even thought we might be God's choice for each other. However, he had a serious heart problem. He suspected he would die soon.

Charlie's love validated me and improved my self-esteem. But after we'd corresponded three and a half months, I received an email from his daughter stating he'd died. Later, she sent his goodbye letter: "You are still going to make some lucky man the best wife in the world. I wish it had been me. But since it isn't, maybe God is getting you ready for the real one."

After this experience, although I had another painful grief to go through, I felt healthier emotionally and spiritually than I had before. God had done some deep inner healing in me.

Some time later, it seemed God guided me back to the singles' site, as if what he had started to do wasn't finished yet. This time, I wrote to Paul and asked him to be my Pen Pal.

Paul replied, "Yes, I would like to be your Pen Pal" and we continued to correspond. Later, I learned he had prayed three years earlier, "Lord, I'm so lonely. I've been a widower for twelve years. The kids are raised and out of the house now and I'm rattling around in this house by myself. Don't you have somebody for me?" (He was retired by then from teaching for 35 years and worked as a landscaper.)

He heard God's answer in his heart, "Yes—but she's not ready for you yet." He accepted that and waited three more years.

Then in desperation, he prayed again. "Please, God, don't you have someone for me? I want a wife who loves God with all her heart and will love me and let me treat her like a gentleman with kindness and respect. Also, please, could she be pretty?"

Within two weeks of that prayer, he received my first email. He didn't know what I looked like because, for some reason, he never saw my profile. We found out we had not used the same web site.

After a few months of correspondence, long enough to assure each other of the sincerity of our faith and to learn much about each others' lives, we were good friends and wanted to meet each other.

So, I drove 1700 miles to visit Paul. He invited me to a Sweet Corn Serenade the first evening. Paul says he fell in love with me when he first saw me coming down the stairs of the motel where he picked me up. (No, the sweet corn didn't sing, but he held my hand and our hearts sang.)

Paul is of Dutch heritage, so we toured a replica of a Dutch village and windmill the next day, eating poffertjes, and trying on Dutch caps. The more time Paul and I spent together, the more we enjoyed it.

We believed God brought us together, although we couldn't quite figure out the connection between two separate singles sites. After a couple other visits back and forth, we married in my home church in Washington before I moved to live in his home in Iowa.

I am grateful God granted my request. My husband, Paul, not only gives me the loving emotional support I need, but appreciates my help. He encourages me to pursue God's calling as a writer and in other things, so I call him my "Barnabas" (after Barnabas, the "Son of Encouragement" in Acts 4:36.) We are united in Christ, growing spiritually as we share our faith intimately with each other. God has replaced our loneliness with joy, friendship and love.

A Small Bio:

Judith Vander Wege was married to her "Pen Pal" Paul Vander Wege for nearly 16 years before he died in 2022. Her writing has been published in several Christian periodicals, take-home papers, compilations and devotional booklets, as well as three books: <u>Rescued by God's Mercy, Songs & Poems From a Yielded Heart, and The Runaway.</u> You can reach her through her website, http://judithvanderwege.com or her email, judith.vw.4hm@gmail.com.

Chapter Nineteen

As octopuses do

My three-year-old son and I walked hand in hand toward the swimming pool one summer afternoon. Anxious, dark thoughts kept me from enjoying the beautiful, sunny day. *How on earth can I manage to get everything done?* I worried silently.

After a short silence in his cheerful chatter, Joshua said, as if in response to my thoughts, "Mom, I wish people had as many arms as octopuses do. Then we could handle everything!" Startled out of my reverie by his pertinent words, I stopped and stared at him. As I pictured myself with eight octopus arms, trying to juggle my responsibilities, I chuckled and felt my tension lessen.

We continued through the park, and I began to smell the apple blossoms and lush green grass. Looking at my precious son, I thanked God for him. New hope rose in my heart. I dismissed anxiety from my mind, remembering that the God who gave me that beloved son has promised to work in everything for my good. Since his grace is sufficient for me, I don't need to "handle everything."

Chapter Twenty

The Ultimate Compliment

Earlier, another three-year-old son, Toby, watched with obvious adoration in his big brown eyes as I put on my makeup, having dressed up to go somewhere. As I finished, I turned and smiled at him. With awe in his voice, he gave me the ultimate compliment, "Oh Mommy! You look Enormous!"

As I hugged my adorable son, I could sense that God also enjoys our praise, even when we get the words mixed up.

Chapter Twenty-One

What now my lord?

"What will I do," I asked my husband, choking back a sob, "when I can no longer tell you about all my little aches and pains?" Lying side by side on our bed, we shared a few quiet moments between visits of relatives. I pulled the soft blanket up around Martin's thin shoulders. *Shame on you, Judy,* I thought, *complaining about allergies while Martin is dying of cancer.* He silently squeezed my hand. This had always been his signal to let me know he understood and it was okay and he loved me. Then, I could no longer hold back the tears.

"What's the matter?" he asked. "Come here." He gathered me into his arms. Stroking my hair and patting my shoulder, he tenderly comforted me as I wept. I answered through my tears, "I want to keep on feeling your arms around me. I want to keep on holding your hand."

Martin silently caressed me until my sobs stopped, then said, "Just hold on to Jesus, Honey." This answer comforted me. It pointed me to the one who can give the most support to a grieving person.

When Martin died on October 14, 2003, God provided a lot of support for me. We had known for ten months that he had cancer. I appreciated that we had time to prepare the will and the order of service together, time to get our finances in order with the help of insurance benefits. We had time to say goodbye.

Family and friends came to our house frequently, especially during the last three and a half months while he was on hospice care. Many let us know they prayed, or brought food, helped in other ways, or sent cards. We had comforting memorial services and pastoral calls. Hugs and expressions of love were abundant.

Yet, I had questions. *What will I do? Why me? Why did he have to die so young? Why didn't God heal him? What did I do wrong?*

Grief hits us all hard sooner or later. We may have the support of friends and family, or may feel abandoned. But no matter how much support there is, questions surface:

What do I do now? Will I be alone the rest of my life, or will God guide me to remarry someday? Will I be strong enough to wait for His choice?

I felt I needed to get my house in order and get my work done so I'd be ready when it is time for me to go home to heaven. But I wondered, *what is the work I'm to do, the purpose for which I was born?* Like Paul, (Philippians 1:21-24), I felt the quandary of wanting to go home, yet feeling I should stay.

Grief, if we will allow the Lord to work through it, provokes questions that can guide us toward the future. *Am I to be one of God's Spokesmen as a writer? I've thought so for 25 years, but sales of manuscripts have been few and far between. Is it a hobby, or a calling? What now, Lord? I want to be used of you as your instrument, your vessel of honor. How? Writing? Music? Songwriting?*

Out of these questions and reveries poured more questions. *Now that he's gone, why am I still here*? Then I prayed, "How can I glorify you, Lord? If I can't glorify you, can't I just come to Heaven now to be with you? Please give me strength to obey you, to show you I love you."

Eventually, a song flowed out of my heart:

"I love you, LORD. You're mine forever. You're my Redeemer, King, and friend.
You've paid the price; your blood has saved me. You gave me life that will never end.
You'll never leave; you'll hold me tight. The devil's lost! You have won the fight.
What now, my LORD? What shall I do to let you know how much I love you?

You gave me peace that I can't fathom, an inner joy in the midst of pain.
I want to be your chosen vessel. "To live is Christ and to die is gain."
You'll lead me on o'er land and sea. To be with you is where I want to be.
What now my LORD? What shall I do? A yielded life shows that I love you."

Since the song was a prayer, God answered me in my heart. Jesus will never leave me nor forsake me. He is my Redeemer, King, and best friend. He will hold on to me and I'll be safe. I felt a peace, knowing I don't need to know all the answers. I just need to remember he makes everything work for good for those who love him. This assurance gave me joy in the midst of pain. The song ended with my yielding to my LORD, Jesus Christ. He is my Master. I realized this is all He wants of me—to yield to Him and obey Him daily as He leads me step by step. A yielded life shows that I trust Jesus, that I am holding on to him. That TRUST is what glorifies him.

As Told to Stories

Chapter Twenty-Tow

A Soul Set Free

By Alexandra Zamora
as told to Judith Vander Wege

"God, if you truly exist, you have to know I am looking for you! I give you time until 6 a.m. tomorrow to appear to me here."   ---Dr. Alexandra Zamora, evangelist, Costa Rica 1985.

Hearing this animated woman tell of her dramatic life change, I thought of the chorus:.

"I believe in miracles, I've seen a soul set free.
Miraculous the change in one redeemed through Calvary."
--- John W. Peterson

Yes, I believe in miracles. Alexandra is one. After a relatively loveless and abusive childhood, she became addicted to drugs and alcohol in her teens and experienced many problems connected with that as years went by.

****

She told me: "I became a model for publicity campaigns, and began a long term relationship with a man from South America. We traveled a lot, always with bodyguards and bulletproof cars. I came to know many public figures, important at an international level. Among these were some whose business was illicit. Life became more difficult with anxieties and problems with the police. The price was high for this lifestyle. Often, after parties, compulsive sobs would overtake me.

"On one of these occasions I picked up a Bible someone had given me years before and took it along on a trip to the Polynesian Islands instead of the usual fashion magazines. On the flight, a passenger I immediately disliked sat beside me. She asked, "Where are you going? Who are you going to see?"

"Upset with her questions, I took out my book to ignore her. To my surprise, she took out a book exactly the same and began to read. She asked, "Are you a Christian?"

"Yes."

"What kind?" she asked.

"Well, Christian." I didn't know there were different theologies among Christians.

"I am too."

"She opened her English Bible and pointed to a text, asking me to find the verse in my Spanish Bible. The verse read, "I, the Lord, command you do not fornicate any more nor commit adultery." What a surprise! How did she know the man I was going to visit was not my husband? I did not talk much more with her during the flight.

"At the Polynesians, my luggage had not come on our plane. The person meeting me took me to the boat to wait for the luggage. The only thing I had to do was read, so I read my Bible all day for fifteen days. Afterward, I fell to my knees in my room asking God to forgive me for being an adulteress, fornicator, alcoholic, liar, and poor mother. Something inside me said: "Why are you asking pardon for that, that's not bad." It was a complicated situation. That day I had my first real encounter with the truth of God. After that trip I returned to Los Angeles, found some friends and went to a gay night club.

"While there, I shared the experience with them. Some began to cry and others were touched. Some began following in God's footsteps. Returning to Costa Rica, even though there was in my heart the idea that maybe there existed a God, I continued in drugs, in my disorderly life, and in expensive parties. My life continued empty.

"One afternoon a man arrived at my door saying, "Alexandra, here are some grams of cocaine."

"I replied: "No. I don't want them. Take them back."

"Some very uncommon thing in me reinforced my will. Around one in the morning while I was resting, a terrible anxiety and desperation for the drug overcame me. I needed to phone the person who supplied me with the drug. But deep within me was the thought that I needed to know if what I was involved in was of Satan. I said to God, "Show me if my life is not in agreement with what you have for me. Tell me if it is of Satan. I need an answer. I ask you that within ten minutes the telephone ring and it be the person that provides me with drugs."

"Exactly ten minutes later the telephone rang. I answered to hear a voice say: "Why have you left me? For whom have you abandoned me?"

"I answered: "For God I have left you. I abandoned you for God."

"She laughed sarcastically. "You'll never be able to leave me, because I am a legion." (Later I learned a legion is a group of demons sent to destroy a person, a family or a town.)

"

"God had granted my request! Supernatural peace captivated me, and I slept peacefully all night. I finally understood the path I'd been on led to death and was contrary to God's will. Since I'd never heard the gospel, I hadn't known the life I lived was sinful.

"I spent Easter Week of 1985 with my family. On Good Friday, my mother brought me some food. I replied, "No, Mommy, but thanks anyway." I said to God, "If fasting is not good, please forgive me, but if it is good, please receive it for my freedom."

"That afternoon I went to the mountain and, while my family maintained silence remembering the crucifixion of Jesus Christ, I talked with Him. "People say you died many years ago. I really don't understand much of that, but if anything that happened was for me, I thank You." Then I began to cry. I was searching for a living God, a God of power.

"Easter Sunday, I returned with my family to their house. That night with my ten-year-old daughter sleeping beside me, I felt I was dying from drug addiction because I'd seen many die and recognized the symptoms. In desperation, I called out to God to reveal himself to me. "I am looking for you, not because I want fame or money. I am looking for you to give you my heart. But I warn you... if I die and go to hell, it is your fault because if you are truly God, you know I am looking for you. I give you time until 6 am tomorrow morning to appear to me here. Don't send me any human to talk to me about you, because I do not trust any human being. If you appear here in this room and free me from those who are after me, from drugs and alcohol, from guilt for having abandoned my loved ones, for having coldness of heart and insensitivity towards others, I promise I will serve you every minute of my life."

"After a prolonged period of crying, I went to sleep. At 6 am I awoke. In a supernatural experience I saw myself flying in a silver airplane that landed on a gray beach. People got off the plane and walked towards some gray caves in the distance. I followed them off the plane, but as I reached the bottom step I realized someone was standing there, dressed in white. It was Jesus Christ! He hugged me, put his arm around my shoulders and led me along the beach, talking to me as we went. His last words to me were "confess I am your Lord." God had visited me just as I had challenged him to do. From that day on, the power of God has broken into my life and I am free, ready to follow God, and have Him touch others through me.

"Never again have I smoked marijuana or cigarettes, drunk liquor or taken cocaine. My heart is transformed. God gave me love, sensitivity, and great compassion toward others. I am repulsed by my former way of living. My daughter, who'd been hurt and mistreated, also came to the feet of Jesus. We talked and forgave one another. Many former friends were visited by the Holy Spirit through my life and God has done marvelous things in them.

"God is interested in your life, too. He loves you. He's alive, is powerful and can free you if you'll only ask him to make you a new person. You can pray this prayer with me: "Heavenly Father, thank you for giving your Son, Jesus Christ, to die on a cross for my sins. I believe in you and give you my life. I invite you to enter into my heart and be

my Savior and Lord. Make my life according to your will. Thank you, Lord. Amen."

Chapter Twenty-Three

Out of the depths

By Gena Lewis as told to Judith Vander Wege

My eyes flew open at the sound of footsteps. *Is he coming?* I stared into the darkness, my heart pounding. *Will he do it again?* I clutched Barky closer, as if a stuffed animal could protect a ten-year-old girl.

A week had passed since that terrible night. Ever since, terror filled me. I'd lie awake in shame wondering why I deserved this. *It must be my fault, since Mom is staying with him.*

Tasting the alcohol had been exciting. And we all played tag, even our step-dad. Then came that terrible moment alone in the bedroom with him … and he took hold of me, and …   <u>This bedroom! I've got to get out of here! He's drinking again and he's coming!</u>

Grabbing my jeans and sweatshirt, I ran to a room under the stairs. I quickly dressed as I heard the stairway door opening, then held my breath. The footsteps came down the stairs proceeding to the bedroom. Watching for my chance, I slipped out the door, up the stairs and outside. I ran until my breath caught in my throat.

"Now what?" I asked Barky, surprised to see him still in my hand.

Looking around at the dark streets, I wondered what to do. A dumpster nearby looked like a good hiding place, so I got in. <u>Phew! How stinky!</u> But it didn't take me long to fall asleep.

Next day, hunger won out over fear and I returned home. But running away became a pattern for my teen-age years, as did rebellion, drinking, and drugs. Each member of our family was trapped in a prison of pain and despair. Life didn't seem worth living. I didn't believe God could forgive or help me. A couple times, I slit my wrists. Often, I drank myself into a stupor.

At fifteen, I finally had a little stability and love when my aunt, then another loving family, took me in until I finished alternative high school.

When David and I married, I had quit drugs but still drank. Alcohol helped me forget my problems and feel outgoing. We partied every weekend the first few years.

Meanwhile, I took our sons to church as soon as they could walk. I watched people "get saved," wishing I could. I thought I had to quit drinking and smoking first. Since I couldn't quit, I felt empty and defeated.

One night, I watched a drama at church. "Jesus" lived, died, and rose again before my eyes. Drawn to the love and mercy of Jesus, I asked him into my heart. I felt the heavy burdens of emotional baggage lifted off my shoulders as I wept.

Yet, life remained a struggle and my spiritual growth was slow. One tremendous step of growth, however, came a few weeks later. Some friends invited us to a party. <u>I'll just visit and not get drunk</u>, I decided. But after one drink "to settle my nerves," I lost control and kept on drinking.

Soon, I could hardly walk. After throwing up in the bathroom, I lay on a sleeping bag in a dark bedroom. For some time, I lay listening to the sounds of the party. <u>I wish someone would come check on me</u>, I thought.

<u>Something's wrong! I can't move my arms or legs! Why aren't they coming?</u> I thought, weeping. <u>These are my best friends!</u>

Soon, it seemed as if I left my aching body and my shame, confusion, and sadness. Light appeared. Bathed in golden sunshine, I felt light as a feather and beautiful as a flower as Jesus held my hand.

Then I heard people talking.

"Is she breathing still? I can't feel her pulse!"

"I could feel warm air from her nose a minute ago, but not now!"

"Oh, don't worry. She'll be OK."

I couldn't answer. They went back to partying and suddenly I felt sorry for them. They tried to find happiness in a bottle, just as I had done. Satan made it look like fun and good, while I lay half dead from alcohol poisoning. But Jesus held my hand and gave me peace the rest of the night.

I learned a lesson about people and alcohol that night. People will fail you sometimes. Especially when alcohol is involved, people are selfish. However, God will never fail you. After this horrible night, I asked God to take control of my life. Amazingly, he has delivered me from this addiction, and later from smoking also, without withdrawal symptoms!

Set free from these addictions, I became more interested in my Bible. The more I studied and applied God's Word to my daily life, the better I felt about my life. With God in control, the empty feelings went away. But David didn't appreciate that I wouldn't party with him anymore. I was in a war to choose between God and my husband. I didn't want our sons, aged five and seven, to grow up with alcoholism and its problems. So I wouldn't compromise. "If you're going to live that kind of life," David said, "I don't want to be part of it." So he moved out.

This broke my heart. But God used it to draw me closer until I gave myself completely to Him and let Him be in charge. From then on, I wanted to do only what pleases God. I prayed to know what I did wrong and what God wanted for me.

Throughout the next weeks, David and I communicated about our problems with the help of counselors and much prayer. Eventually, he moved back home and God gave me a fresh, new love for him greater than when we first got married. Eventually God developed faith in him, also.

Now I know that consistently committing every problem to the LORD is the way to peace, joy and fulfillment.

Articles

Chapter Twenty-Four

What is a Christian?

What does it mean to be a Christian? The world has a lot of ideas about Christians, but the title simply means "follower of Christ." Those of us who believe what the Bible says about Jesus Christ want to follow him, to be in relationship with him, because we understand he is the one our loving Creator sent to rescue us from Satan.

From the beginning of humankind, when the first humans disobeyed God, every human being has sinned except Jesus Christ. We are unable to live sinless lives because Satan has captured humanity. But Jesus, the Son of the only true Living God, who is fully divine and also fully human, came to this earth from Heaven to set the captives free. When Jesus died on the cross and then rose again, he broke the padlock on our prison. Now we have the choice. We can stay in that stinky prison and just exist, or we can follow him out of the prison and experience the peace and joy of forgiveness and have a purpose that makes life worth living even when circumstances are difficult. When we follow him, we may stumble at times. We may not always act the way he teaches us to act. But if we believe he is who he says he is in the Bible, then he will help us in our weaknesses, forgive all our sins, and teach us how to live the way God intended us to live when he created us. He forgives us and cleanses us if we admit our sin to him and ask his forgiveness.

God is good, holy, pure, merciful, everywhere present, all-knowing, all-powerful, three persons (Father, Son, and Holy Spirit) in one God. He created us and all that exists including the vast universe and everything Science has discovered and much that has not yet been discovered or properly understood. Everything was good when he created it, but then Lucifer, one of the most glorious angels he created, became prideful and rebelled against his Creator. He and the angels who followed him came to earth and tempted people to disobey, deceiving them to fall into his trap. Lucifer's rebellion and the resultant disobedience to God of all humankind is the reason for the mess in the world (evil, sickness, heartache and pain and every other evil.)

God has given us a way out of that mess. The way is Jesus Christ.

God loves us and wants us to follow Jesus. But he won't force us. He has given us the choice to believe or not. If we do believe and receive Jesus Christ as Savior and Lord, accepting his forgiveness for our sins, we are adopted into God's family and allowed the privilege of working in his family business. The benefits are wonderful, both now and eternally. We have the peace of knowing we are forgiven and accepted by God, we are given the ability to live in love with Jesus and through him to love others, we don't have to live in constant fear or remain trapped in bitterness or addictions. We often experience his healing power or other miracles. His Holy Spirit guides us to live a life pleasing to our Lord.

If you have comments, feel free to email me at judith.vw.4hm@gmail.com.

Chapter Twenty-Five

Christian Spirituality is Distinctive

This is a paper I wrote for a final exam in college In 2014

Spirituality is a term popular in our world today. It can apply to most anything whether "a sociocultural movement, an interest group, or a particular cause or concern" (Chan, 15) as well as to the religious life. It can apply to yoga, meditation, 12-step programs, long walks, et cetera.

Christian spirituality, on the other hand, applies to the truth of the "Christian story revolving around the life, death and resurrection of Jesus of Nazareth," (Chan, 15). Theology is the study of God (specifically, of that Christian story) and spirituality is the way we live when we believe that story. The Christian may do some of the same things as 'secular' spiritual people: exercise, meditate (Christians meditate on the scriptures), attend 12-step programs to aid with emotional healing, take long walks, et cetera, but the focus is different. Christians do these things as good stewards (caring for the body) and praising the Triune God (especially for who Christ is and what his life, death and resurrection has done in and for our lives).

Christian spirituality should lead one to live "life under a certain pattern of discipline" according to Chan (190). Prayer and Bible reading/study are essential. This keeps our communication open between us and God. Since 'being a Christian' means living in relationship with the holy, omniscient, omnipotent, omnipresent God who created us, it stands to reason that we would want to communicate with that One. We have been adopted into God's family through the payment of Christ's death and resurrection, therefore we can act like children of a beloved Father/Mother, expressing our needs, wishes, hurts, or joys, and hearing the Parent's teachings, encouragements, instructions, warnings, and expressions of love. Reading and meditation on the Bible and praying are that communication.

Tony Jones says, "The goal of Christian Spirituality is to be enlivened by God's Spirit" (26). God is the initiator of the relationship. "It is God's Spirit who gives us spiritual life; it is not ours to attain, achieve, or earn" (27). God brings us into relationship and we respond. I am reminded of the beautiful old hymn which we sang in the Lutheran church when I was a child:

"I sought the Lord, and afterward I knew He moved my soul to seek him, seeking me. It was not I that found, O Saviour true. No, I was found of thee.

"Thou didst reach forth thy hand and mine enfold; I walked and sank not on the storm-vexed sea. 'Twas not so much that I on thee took hold as thou, dear Lord, on me.

"I find, I walk, I love, but O the whole of love is but my answer, Lord, to thee;

For thou wert long beforehand with my soul. Always thou lovedst me."

                              --- by George Whitefield Chadwick, 1854-1931

My favorite quote from class notes about Christian Spirituality is: "Christian Spirituality is how I, a sinner-saint, live in this world in relation to others and in relation to the Triune God."   ---Jacqueline Smallbones

The things that make spirituality specifically Christian are:

1. Christian spirituality is Trinitarian. God (not the "god within" as gnostics and new agers say, but an Almighty, merciful, all-knowing force outside of us) comes in and animates our lives, coming as a parent to adopt us through the atonement and redemption of Jesus Christ, the only-begotten Son, through the power of the Holy Spirit. The Holy Spirit remains with us to convict of sin, empower us to live according to God's will, to strengthen, encourage, heal, guide and sustain us.

2. Christian spirituality is theologically grounded. Theology establishes the framework for spirituality. We want to be shaped by the Biblical understanding of Father, Son, and Holy Spirit. Also, we need a good vocabulary for this, because words shape us.

3. Christian spirituality is about practicing virtues and acts of piety such as praying, giving alms, and fasting, which Jesus assumed we would do.

4. Christian spirituality is transformative; it will change us. We are called to live life in such a way that we become transformed, (not conformed to this world, but) become like Christ. (see Rom.12:2, 1Pet.1:13-16, Eph. 4:22-24, Col.3;12-17, NRSV).

5. Christian spirituality is both personal and corporate. That is why we worship together and pray corporate prayers.

6. Christian spirituality includes passion and desire. Saints like Catherine of Sienna were passionate about loving God with their whole being. Martin Luther must have been passionate about the truth of justification by grace through faith as he

protested against the abuses of the Roman Catholic Church. The five missionaries told about in *Through Gates of Splendor* (1957) by Elizabeth Elliott were passionate about taking the Gospel to Ecuador.

I know these six points (and the other things I've said so far) are true because of sixty years of reading and studying the Bible and through experience, confirmed through this and other classes at Northwestern College.

My concept of God has changed through the years. As a child, I began learning about God in Sunday school. I have a vivid memory of the day my first grade teacher looked me in the eye and told me, "Jesus loves you." Soon, I began learning the song of the same title. Thus began my concept of God, and it made me wonder how to reach this one who loved me. I felt lonely and wanted someone to look me frequently in the eye and speak lovingly to me. My parents were too busy to do that.

When I was nine years old, we moved from Wisconsin to Minnesota, and became more involved in a small church in the tiny town of Kingston. That fall, our family attended their sister church's Evangelistic services for a week. At the end of the week, I waited for my parents to exit the church. When they shook the Evangelist's hand, I overheard my parents tell him, "We're so glad we came to know the Lord this week." At that moment, it seemed I could hear Jesus whisper into my right ear, "I want to be personal to you, too. Do you say 'yes' or 'no'?"

I said 'yes' in my heart, wondering if anything would be different. The next Sunday, I wondered how the sermon could be so interesting when I'd been so bored previous Sundays. It seemed as if a light had been turned on in my soul, and I could understand spiritual things I'd never thought of before. After that, I enjoyed going to the adult Bible studies, and other things at church. I wasn't so lonely because I believed Jesus was with me. My parents made changes in their lives and started family devotions, which I loved. When they said we had to get rid of our comic books I was surprised, but glad to know they were serious about the new spirituality we had come to experience. I diligently read my Bible my grandparents gave me that Christmas. (I thought God must be like my Grandpa, who seemed to love me unconditionally.)

When our family went to a Palermo Brothers concert, I wished I could sing and play gospel music like them to show my love for the Lord. Shortly thereafter, my parents bought me an accordion and started me in accordion lessons. This seemed like a miracle and an assurance of both their and God's love. My concept of God was growing into a strong faith in a loving God, aided by answers to prayers such as "help me find my glasses." Through high school, this faith drew me to recommit my life to Christ and try to live an obedient life.

But as I grew older, life grew more complicated. My parents had lost their farm and were hurt and depressed, so quit family devotions and didn't talk much to me. It became more difficult to know what decisions to make and to know how to live right. Although my concept of Christ Jesus was biblical, I had trouble believing God the Father loved me. My earthly father seemed distant and quiet, whether from shyness or depression or, (as I thought), lack of interest in me as a person. Therefore, my concept of

God the Father was that he wasn't really interested in my daily life. When troubles happened and God didn't answer my prayers the way I thought was right, I felt abandoned. That feeling led to anger, and I made some wrong choices, disobeying my Father God.

As I suffered the painful consequences of my disobedience, what hurt the most was that I knew I had hurt the heart of God. I felt the discipline was just, but also merciful. Then I realized that—since God kept the promise about discipline—God would also keep promises for blessings. I repented, and got into a small church that ministered healing to me, especially in their small group meetings. As they laid hands on me and prayed scripture over me, it felt like God was speaking directly to my heart through them. One of the scriptures meaningful to me at that time was when Jesus told his disciples "the Father himself loves you," (John 16:27, RSV). My concept of God was changing.

The worship services were also very meaningful in this charismatic church. As the worship leader led us in songs and prayers, it seemed as if he ushered us into the very throne room of heaven. One Sunday as we worshiped and as I wept in sorrow over my sins and my problems, it felt like Jesus gently picked me up (in the spirit) and carried me over the threshold into the Holy of Holies, and set me on my heavenly Father's lap. This was such a healing thing for my emotions!

People in this church had encouraged me to read five Psalms a day, which I did diligently for at least four years. Through their ministry and the Psalms, God convinced me of his "Father/Mother" love more completely than I had ever known it before. I also gained more of a confidence of being led by the Holy Spirit.

I realize that if I don't have a good concept of God, I can't feel close (relationally) to God. When I felt abandoned, I didn't feel like obeying. But I still knew God was almighty and sovereign. When I realized my heavenly Father still loved me and was mercifully calling me back into his arms, I rejoiced and clung to him, and begged the Holy Spirit; "work in me that which is pleasing to you, and complete the good work you've begun in me," (See Phil.2:13 and 1:6, NRSV). Because of love, I wanted to stay in the right relationship with my maker, my redeemer and comforter.

Bible Study, with meditation and memorization as well as reading, is extremely important for gaining a proper concept of and living in a meaningful relationship with God. God is holy (Psalms 22:3, Isaiah 6:3, I Peter 1:15), just (Ezra 9:15, Romans8:4), all-powerful (Gen.17:1, Rev.19:6), omniscient (Rev.2:2, Job 23:10, Psalms103:14, Mt.6:8), merciful(Jonah 4:2, Luke 6:36), loving (John 3:16, Rev.1:5, Rom. 5:8), and Triune (Gen.1:2/John 1:1,14:10,16,15:26). Jesus Christ is God the Son who came to save us from our sins, (Luke 1:32-35, Mt.1:21, Rom.8:3-4, Ephesians 2:4-8). The Holy Spirit bears witness to Jesus (John 15:26), convicts of sin (John16:8), is the guarantee of our inheritance (Ephesians 1:13-14), empowers us to do God's will (Rom.15:19, Rom.8:26), and guides us (John16:13). This is a small sample of the verses that tell what God is like.

Bibliography: Chan, Simon. *Spiritual Theology: a Systematic Study of the Christian Life*. Downers Grove, Ill.: InterVarsity Press, 1998.

Elliot, Elizabeth. *Through Gates of Splendor*. Hendrickson Publishers, 1957.

Jones, Tony. *The Sacred Way: Spiritual Practices for Everyday Life*. Grand Rapids, MI: Zondervan, 2005.

NRSV. *The New Oxford Annotated Bible, NRSV with Apocrypha*. New York: Oxford University Press, 2001.

Service Book and Hymnal. USA: The American Evangelical Lutheran Church, et all, 1958-63. Page 473.

Chapter Twenty-Six

Embrace the Call

I used to watch a show on TV called *Mission Impossible.* At the beginning of each episode, a group of people would receive a tape recording from a mysterious, unseen 'boss' who had recorded instructions for them. The tape began, "Your mission, if you should choose to accept it, is …."

They had a choice. Of course they always accepted it, or else there wouldn't be a show. And it was always something urgent and beneficial to mankind.

Likewise, we Christians have a choice to accept or reject the call of God on our lives. Our mission is also important and beneficial to mankind. Jesus asked his disciples at one point to pray for laborers for the harvest. He has work for us to do.

Each of us has a unique mission in life. We are not all called to be writers anymore than we are all called to be foreign missionaries, but each of us has a unique place in God's Kingdom. We don't all receive the same call, but the same steps apply. When Isaiah received his call, (Isaiah 6) he first had an encounter with God which impressed him with God's holiness and "above-ness." He saw God as Almighty and worthy of worship. Secondly, he was impressed with his own sin and unworthiness. Thirdly, he received forgiveness through the angel touching his lips with a coal from the altar (a piece of sacrificed lamb). Then he heard the call "Whom shall I send and who will go for us?" Isaiah then volunteered to be sent wherever God wished to send him.

If we are obedient disciples of Jesus Christ, we will follow these steps. We must see God as holy and worthy of our worship and obedience, repent of our sin, accept forgiveness, and respond to whatever call God extends to us.

As I read Isaiah 6:8, it seems that Isaiah was eager to be chosen. I think this is the case for most people who have truly had an encounter with Christ, become aware of the depravity of their sin, and truly accepted forgiveness. We believe Christ, the sacrificial lamb, took our sins upon himself so we could be clothed in righteousness. We embrace his call out of gratitude and joy for what he has done for us. We want to do something in return for him.

Embracing God's call includes:

1. Receiving the call as a choice God extends to us---"Who will go for us?" He knows who is equipped for what, because he made us.

2. Hearing and understanding the call—*I can do that, I'd like to serve God that way.*

3. Accepting the call—Here am I, Lord, send me!"

4. Obeying the call—continuing to persevere in doing what you believe God has called you to do, even when it gets difficult. For writers, this means even when editors and agents seem to reject everything you send, even when you are tired of sitting at a computer, even when your computer gives you fits, even when you can't sleep because 'things you should write' keep going through your

mind, even when you get lonely because you are too busy working at writing to socialize with family or friends.

5. We must carry out the call in the power of the Holy Spirit. I'm so glad we don't have to do it alone. But this takes effort to be in tune with the Holy Spirit. It takes much Bible reading, study, memorizing, research, and constant prayer (without ceasing). He promises his guidance, but we need to ask for it and then take time to listen.

6. As disciples, we also should rejoice in and embrace the call he has given. A call from God is a treasure, a privilege. As adopted children of God, we are given the opportunity to take part in God's family business. He has loved us and cared for us, so, out of gratitude, we want to do his bidding, to put forth the effort to do his will in furthering his Kingdom.

In summary, to embrace the call is to respond to our Lord in love, to rejoice in the opportunity to be of service to him, to treasure it and treasure the gifts he gives to help us carry it out, to delight in carrying out the 'mission' offered to us "if we should choose to accept it.

Chapter Twenty-Seven

They Chose to Die

How would you feel if the one in power told you to give up all your Christian customs and turn your back on the God who not only gave you life but made that life worth living, full of joy and peace? If he tried to keep you from fulfilling your part of the covenant with your God, to force you to worship someone else, and also tortured your fellow believers, would you fight back? I can see in the historical setting of the books of Maccabees a strong resemblance both to Hitler's holocaust of the Jews and to persecution that is still going on in many parts of the world against Christians.

According to Robert Doran, "Antiochus III affirmed the right of the Jews to live according to their ancestral religion."(NIB 6). But Antiochus IV who came to the Seleucid throne in 175 BCE had other ideas. He called himself *Epiphanes* which means *god (or Zeus) manifest*, in other words *god in the flesh*. Naturally, this name itself would grate against the beliefs of any dedicated to worshiping the one true God, although it may not have bothered polytheists much.

There were many factions in Jerusalem at this time. Some were in favor of the spread of Greek culture (Hellenization) and others weren't. Antiochus IV Epiphanes bestowed the job of high priest on the one who bribed him the most, so a wealthy man got the job. This high priest, Jason, renamed Jerusalem as "Antioch-at-Jerusalem" and built a Greek gymnasium which he thought every decent Greek city should have. Many were in favor of this "progress," but others believed it was wrong.

Then Menelaus offered Antiochus a larger bribe and became high priest instead of Jason. This Menelaus apparently betrayed his own people, according to Hauer & Young. "After Rome thwarted an unsuccessful attempt to add Egypt to Antiochus Epiphanes' empire, Antiochus salved his ego by entering Jerusalem on the Sabbath, slaughtering innocent people, and looting the temple, with the full cooperation of Menelaus (H & Y, 217).

It was 80,000 Jews he slaughtered (Eerdmans, 437). The NIB says this was in order to squelch a revolt or factional war between Jason and Menelaus (NIB,10). Perhaps a better explanation was that he was a madman who thought himself god and/or was demon-possessed.

According to Eerdmans, the 11th chapter of Daniel prophesied the history of the Greek Empire accurately in the 6th century BCE (Eerdmans, 437). "If the possibility of genuine prediction in prophecy is allowed, the book can be taken as it stands, as the record of the life and visions of Daniel himself. Only if it is denied is one bound to conclude that the book cannot be earlier than the 2nd century BC" (Eerdmans, 430).

The section we are examining, 1 Maccabees 1:41-64, occurred in 167 BCE. The massacre and plunder of the temple had taken place two years earlier. After another massacre, Verse 41 says "the king wrote to his whole kingdom that all should be one people, and that all should give up their particular customs" (NOAB, 204) and accept "his religion" (verse 43).

He outlawed the practice of circumcision (the Jewish sign of the covenant), forbade them to offer sacrifices in their sanctuary or to keep their Sabbaths and festivals. He even tried to force them to eat foods they believed God had forbidden them to eat. "They were to make themselves abominable by everything unclean and profane, so that they would forget the law and change all the ordinances" (verses 48b-49, NOAB 205). He brought in idol worship, destroyed their books of the covenant and set up a "desolating sacrilege" in the temple. If anyone disobeyed the king, he was killed and so were the babies they sealed with the sign of the covenant.

The Gentiles and many of the Israelites accepted Antiochus IV Epiphanes' religion, but others were resolved to remain faithful to God. "They chose to die rather than to be defiled—or to profane the holy covenant" (v.63).

What would you do? Would you conform to paganism or false religion forced upon you? Or would you die rather than deny your LORD? (Many in the middle east and China and Africa are making this decision even today.) 1 & 2 Maccabees continue on to tell about the revolt of the Hasmonean family. "The Maccabees fought according to their own convictions to keep alive the worship of the God of Israel. For that, their name will be remembered" (NIB, 178).

In the reflections at the end of the commentary on 1 Maccabees, Doran says "the author emphasizes that God does act faithfully to the people if they attempt to follow

God's commandments" (NIB, 178). Many stories of Christian martyrs vouch to the truth of that (see <u>Foxe's Book of Martyrs</u> or <u>Jesus Freaks by dc Talk</u> and the <u>Voice of the Martyrs.</u> They may be killed, but God gives them grace to endure the suffering before they enter eternal life of joy and peace. There in heaven, they will never suffer again.

Works cited:

NIB: Robert Doran, <u>New Interpreter's Bible</u>, Vol. IV. Nashville: Abingdon Press, 1996.

NOAB: <u>The New Oxford Annotated Bible,</u> NRSV with Apocrypha. Michael Coogan, ed., Mary Chilton Callaway: 1 & 2 Maccabees. New York: Oxford University Press, 2001.

H&Y: <u>An Introduction to the Bible: a Journey into Three Worlds</u>. 7th ed. Christian E. Hauer & William A. Young. NJ: Pearson Prentice Hall, 2008.

<u>Eerdman's Handbook to the Bible.</u> Edited by David and Pat Alexander. Grand Rapids, MI: William B. Eerdman's Publishing Company, American Edition 1992.

Chapter Twenty-Eight

You are the Man!

If you had to reprimand a King, how would you go about doing it? It must have taken a lot of courage for Nathan the Prophet to confront King David about his sin. Not only was David a highly respected man, but powerful enough to execute anyone who made him angry. He had already had a man killed to cover up his covetousness and adultery. What would he do to the one who uncovered it and accused him of murder? "The thing David had done was evil in the eyes of the LORD." (NIV and NRSV soften it, but this is the accurate way to translate this verse, according to The New Interpreter's Bible (NIB Vol. II. 1285)).

Therefore "The LORD sent Nathan to David" to tell him this and Nathan obeyed (2 Sam. 11:27b-12:15, NRSV). We can learn something from this: When the LORD tells us to do something, we can expect he will equip us for that task. I'm sure Nathan's courage came from the LORD. The inspiration to use the parable of the "Ewe Lamb" also came from the LORD.

In the book, The Language of Love, Smalley & Trent use this parable as an example of an emotional word picture which has the power to change a person's heart (LOL 49-54). It certainly gripped David's emotions! In anger, he declared the man in the story deserved to die and must make four-fold restitution. The Prophet Nathan skillfully caught King David's attention with this emotional word picture, and it changed his heart.

Parable is defined as "a method of speech in which moral or religious truth is illustrated from the analogy of common experience" (Davis 568). It is similar to a simile or metaphor, but is a longer story. Jesus often spoke in parables also in the New Testament. When truth is conveyed through a parable, it "adheres to the memory much more than a plain didactic statement would do" (568). Also, the person often responds (as David did) before realizing that he himself is the character in the story.

Commentators further define this parable (which is a small section of the single literary unit called the *Succession Narrative* or *Court History of David)* as a "*juridical parable*, which intentionally disguises a real-life situation in order to draw a guilty party into passing judgment on himself" (NIB, 1292).

I & II Samuel are listed as two historical books in the Christian Bible. But in the Jewish Bible they are combined into one book as part of the Nevi'im or former prophets. They tell about the beginning of the monarchy in Israel and it's first two kings, Saul and David. Samuel is named for the prophet Samuel, the main character in the first few chapters of I Samuel who anointed Saul and later David to be King over Israel. Chapters 16-31 and II Samuel focus on David. First and second Samuel is a literary masterpiece, according to NOAB notes (NRSV 398). "Who will succeed David" is the story question of The Succession Narrative (chapters 9-20). It is an example of the literary form called the Hebrew short story or novella. Nathan's parable is a word picture within a scene in a novella within a larger narrative called the Deuteronomistic History within our Old Testament and the Jewish Bible).

The historical setting for this scene is about 980 BCE in Jerusalem. David had been king first over Judah, and then over the entire nation of Israel about 30 years and controlled most of the land between Egypt and the Euphrates River. Most of their enemies were subdued by this time, but his army still fought the Ammonites.

Jewish tradition attributes authorship of 2 Samuel to the Prophets Nathan and Gad. It is "reasonable to assume" the book was completed before 722 BCE (Nelson 505). It is easy to believe Nathan wrote at least this section, but "a few notes may have been added after the division of the monarchy." The author used documents dating back to David's reign in 1010-970 and earlier, including eyewitness accounts, and a later editor wove memoirs together (505).

Other scholars disagree about who wrote 2 Samuel and when. McCarter discusses ancient texts (AB vol.8, p3-8), concluding the Septuagint is more accurate than the Masoretic Text, citing studies by Thenius, Wellhausen, and S.R. Driver. This was confirmed when ancient Hebrew manuscripts were discovered at Qumran in 1952. However, the earliest known manuscript of 2 Samuel 11:2 through 1 Kings 11 is from a late translation which may have gone through several revisions. This is one reason for the controversy.

McCarter explains Noth's Hypothesis which says in essence: During the exile after 586 BCE, a single Deuteronomistic Historian looked at past history in relation to the law, and compiled Deuteronomy through 2 Kings (AB vol.9, 4-5). He added editorial notes to help show that Israel's troubles were due to disobedience. He used the extensive sources available for David's reign, so didn't need to editorialize much there.

Another scholar, Cross, thought the primary edition of the history was written during the time of King Josiah, to support his reform. McCarter also believes it was written before the exile, especially chapters 1-5 and 9-20 of I Samuel.

"You are the man!" Nathan told the King. Then, in David's reaction we see why he is still called a "man after God's own heart."(Acts 13:22). He humbly agrees with Nathan and confesses his sin. Perhaps it is almost a relief to have it out in the open. In Psalm 32, David wrote, "While I kept silence, my body wasted away (Psalm 32:3). Because David sincerely repents, Nathan proclaims God's forgiveness, but informs David he will still bear the consequences of his sins. David admits to God that he has "sinned and done what is evil in your sight, so that you are justified in your sentence and blameless when you pass judgment"(Psalm 51:4, NRSV). He knew he didn't deserve God's love. Later verses show him as a broken man: (II Sam.12:16, 13:31, 37, 39, 15:26, 30, 16:10-12, 18:4-5, 18:33-19:4). He knew the evil that befell his family afterward was at least partially his fault.

In Psalm 51, David pours out his heart to God begging for mercy and cleansing. He must have remembered in fear that "the spirit of the LORD departed from Saul" (I Sam.16:14) for he asks "Do not cast me away from your presence, and do not take your holy spirit from me"(Psalm 51:11). That would be the ultimate punishment, for the relationship with God is certainly more important than earthly possessions or kingdoms or anything else.

David's "broken spirit; a broken and contrite heart" (Psalm 51:17) is a sacrifice acceptable to God, and God forgave him. Then he was overwhelmed by a realization of the awesome love of God. *Even though I've failed him miserably, he loves me! Although my sin is evil and wicked, an atrocious affront to his promises, yet he forgives me!"* In Psalm 32, David testifies to the joy of this forgiveness. I think he loves the Lord even more after his terrible sin because he who is forgiven much loves much.

Many of us can relate to David. If we have coveted, taken something which didn't belong to us, violated a trust, tried to cover up our sin, then we are just as guilty as he. Yet, God loves us! How amazing that he loves us when we fail to keep our part of the covenant! He freely offers forgiveness to us. All we need to do is agree with him about our sin and repent when he says, "You are the man!"

Chapter Twenty-Nine

Running the race

Read Hebrews 12:1-3

"Let us fix our eyes on Jesus, the author and perfecter of our faith,...so that [we] will not grow weary and lose heart," (Heb. 12:2a & 3b, NIV).

As a Christian writer, I have often grown weary and become discouraged. Besides the struggle to express thoughts and research in a clear way, marketing is difficult. Rejection letters are a normal part of the job. Someone told me, "When you have enough rejection letters to paper your wall, then you are a real writer."

The idea is that a 'real' writer can't not write. A real writer doesn't quit, but perseveres in his/her calling. A real writer keeps 'running the race.'

Hebrews 12:1 says that because we are surrounded by witnesses, we should throw off hindrances and besetting sins, running "the race marked out for us." Witnesses could be angels, demons, or humans (on earth or heaven). We are often hindered and tempted to quit, yet we want to complete the task or mission God marked out for us.

How can we overcome discouragement and persevere to the end? We can't by our own power. But if we focus on Jesus, thinking about what we've learned about him through the Bible, Sunday School and church, and trusting him, he will encourage us and guide us to write the messages he has called us to write, or to do whatever he has called us to do.

Prayer: Thank you, Jesus, for your encouragement and strength to "run the race."

Prayer Focus: THOSE DISCOURAGED IN THEIR WORK.

Thought for the Day: Focusing on Jesus gives us courage to complete his calling.

Chapter Thirty

Journey to Intimacy: A Road of Questions

Scene One: A blond-haired, seven-year-old girl stands alone on a small hill on a farm in Wisconsin, looking around at a meadow of daisies behind the house, at a huge garden on the other side near the barn, and at the farm place of her aunt and uncle to the west across the road.

Who am I? Why am I here? Do I belong in this family? I don't look like my mom or dad like my sisters do. Am I adopted? Where do I belong?

Scene Two: In a Wisconsin church basement that spring, several Sunday School classes have sung "Jesus Loves Me" together, and now sit in separate circles. The first grade teacher looks at Judy and says, "Jesus loves <u>you</u>!"

Who is Jesus?

Scene Three: Nine and a half years old, Judy stands in the dark outside a Minnesota church after a series of evangelistic meetings, watching people shake an Evangelist's hand, hearing her parents tell him, "We're so glad we found the Lord this week."

Suddenly, she senses Jesus whispering into her right ear, "I want to be personal to you, too. Do you say 'yes' or 'no?' "

"Yes!" she says, eagerly, then looks around at the empty darkness. *Did Jesus really speak to me, or is it only my imagination?*

Scene Four*:* Two days later in the Sunday morning church service, Judy listens intently to the sermon with a surprised look on her face.

I can understand the sermon! How did he get so interesting all of a sudden?

Narrator: The light had been turned on in my soul. From the time I said "yes" to Jesus, he began to make himself known to me. I now knew at least a part of who I am --- a child of God who belongs in his family, through his Son, Jesus Christ, Thus began my spiritual journey.

The journey seemed exciting and smooth for a while, studying the Bible with grown-ups on Wednesday nights, learning at Sunday school and church. Knowing Jesus promised to be with me always, I didn't feel so lonely now. I liked the change in my parents, who now made a point to have family devotions with us, loving the time they now spent with us.

Scene 5: In a large auditorium, two men sing a Gospel concert, accompanying them-selves on guitar and accordion. Judy sits in rapt attention with her family, her face glowing. *I wish I could do that. Could I, Lord? What is your plan for my life?*

Narrator: A dream was born in my heart the night I heard the Palermo Brothers. I wanted to play and sing gospel music like they did to show my love for Jesus. An accordion salesman happened to stop by the next week. What a surprise when my parents, who didn't have extra money lying around, bought one for me and started me on lessons. I decided they must love me more than I had thought. The next three years my self-esteem grew as I learned to play.

Scene 6: A door slams in Kingston, Minnesota. A thirteen-year-old runs across the large back yard to the river where her tree awaits. Sitting in the branches, she cries, writes poetry, and prays. *Why am I here? Does anybody care that I'm alive?*

Narrator: The peace of the home had been disrupted by the loss of our farm two years earlier when the landlord wanted immediate full payment instead of rent. Family devotions had ceased.

The girls in our small school were too boy crazy to have time for me, and the boy I liked had moved away. Mom was too busy and Dad too depressed to give me individual attention. I was jealous of my sisters. It helped to pray, but I also wanted someone I could see and touch to care about me.   Eighth grade was a miserable year.

The following year when I started High School in the larger town of Litchfield, I began to feel much happier. I'd learned at Bible Camp the previous summer that smiles help a person make friends. So I smiled up and down the halls, thankful for the greater variety of classmates from which to choose friends, becoming fairly close with three girls. I loved band, orchestra, choir, and enjoyed most classes. Wednesdays, we had release time for religious instruction at the church of our choice, which was meaningful and enjoyable. Most questions I had in the four years of high school, I could answer. This part of my journey seemed fairly smooth.

Scene 7: A nursing student sits by the phone, trying to concentrate on studying while tears hit the page. *Why didn't he show up for our date? Why doesn't he call?*

Narrator: I had met Keith on a blind date and "fell head over heels in love" with his brown eyes and suave manner. We dated, but it was a stormy relationship. Keith often kissed me like he loved me, then didn't call or come over for a long time. He made dates which he didn't keep. About the time I thought I could get over him, he'd call again, date me again, tell me about girls he made out with. I suspected he was emotionally ill, but figured my love could help him get well. I begged God to make him love me, let him marry me, all the time expecting a 'no' answer.

Scene 8: Location, Deeper Life Bible Camp. A junior high counselor prays in the darkness alone by the lake: After many tears, she says, "Lord, you know I love Keith. But I love you more. If it is a choice between you and Keith, then I choose you."

Narrator: After wrestling with God, then submitting to him, peace enveloped my heart. I felt reassured of God's leading on my journey. However, a year later, Keith called again. I didn't plan to see him, but he was in the hospital, wanting my company. So I went. "I want you to meet my friend," he said. "You'd be just right for him."

"What makes you think he would want your cast-off?" I retorted. Yet, he told me to come the next night when his friend would also come. I did. That's how I met my first husband. Dating him seemed comforting and peaceful after a storm; it seemed God worked through Keith to give me a nice friend—possibly a nice husband.

Yes, he was a nice husband-- for twelve years. My self-esteem grew as wife, mother, and Bible Study leader. Then he became depressed and hardly spoke to me anymore. Years later as I tried to figure out why our marriage failed, I wondered if I'd been disobedient to God in marrying him. *Was it wrong to go see Keith and follow his advice after I had told Jesus I chose him instead? Was it like giving up an idol only to take it back again? And had my husband become an idol to me, more important than Jesus in my life?*

Scene 9: Thirty-four-year-old woman sits at table, writing. It's past midnight. The children are sleeping. Husband is not home yet. She writes furiously for several minutes, then stops, weeping. *Why, Lord? Why won't he tell me what's wrong? Why can't we discuss it? Why won't he go to a counselor with me? And why is her car in front of the office this late at night?* She blows her nose, wipes her eyes, reads in the Bible, then writes again, calmly this time.

Narrator: The act of writing night after night proved therapeutic. It helped to pour out my feelings on paper, then turn them all over to God in a written prayer at the end. Then I could go back to bed and sleep. The words were an attempt to make sense of what was happening to my life, to our relationship, and to figure out what to do about it. By the fourth year of my husband's depression, it became clear to me that the reason he was depressed was that he felt trapped in our marriage, in love with someone else.

Scene 10: Thirty-seven-year-old wife and mother sits weeping at the piano. She plays at random until a pattern forms. Then it appears she is listening to someone sing, although no other person is seen in the room.

Comfort

Let me sing a song to you; let me know if you are feeling blue.

Brush those tears away. Lift your eyes and pray.

I will be your friend, love you to the end. For I came to save you from the tyranny of sin.

Give your heart to me. Life abundantly is what I will give you

when you trust in me to set you free.

I will wipe away your tears; perfect love will cast out all your fears.

Yes, I gave my life, just to end your strife.

When you come to me gold is what I see.

I know you are precious and I want you to be mine.

Clouded now by sin, dirt and dross within. Yield to my refining.

When the trials are done, how you will shine.

1980

Narrator: After hearing Jesus sing to me, I felt comforted and hung on for another year. I'd begun a correspondence course through Christian Writers Guild, encouraged by a friend who had seen my journal. I wrote monthly devotionals for the church newsletter that year, and sold my first article and series of devotionals. Years earlier I had prayed to be used by God, yearning to reach someone other than "church people" with the Gospel. Now it seemed hopeful God would answer my prayer by using me as his instrument through writing.

Scene 11: Woman answers telephone, then hears the words: "What do you mean he's not in town? He's supposed to be here right now! This wedding has been planned for months!"

"I'm sorry. No, I don't know how to reach him." Woman hangs up the phone and drops to her knees. "Dear God! Is he going crazy? How could he forget this? He's always been dependable!"

Narrator: My husband had begun taking days off every week to go out of town alone. My heartache and suspicions were compounded by worry that he would become mentally ill if I didn't set him free. About that time, a fellow musician in our Old Time Fiddlers group began asking me questions about Christianity. I felt useful trying to help him understand and accept the love of God. But being so love-starved myself for the past five years, I was too vulnerable for this to be a safe friendship. He began telling me I was beautiful, which no one had ever done before, and also seemed to enjoy hearing my opinions on things. Soon I fell into the slimy pit of adultery with a "recovering" drug addict and alcoholic. When I told my husband I thought we should get divorced, I hoped he would argue, but instead --- as I expected --- a relieved look appeared on his face and he told me he never had loved me with his whole heart. So after seventeen years of marriage and three children, we separated and divorced.

The "recovering" addict/alcoholic never did recover. I did marry him, thinking that would help, but it didn't. The extremely stressful three years with him became increasingly dangerous. When he tried to choke me to death, I took my counselor's advice to separate, then divorced him. But though things had became worse on the outside, my inner being had began to grew more healthy. At a Youth Conflicts Seminar, I'd realized how sinful my heart looked to God. The adultery had grown out of sinful attitudes such as pride, selfishness, bitterness, judgmental criticism and self-righteousness. When I agreed with God about my sin and repented, I finally understood the grace of forgiveness. Questions which I had formerly directed into thin air, I now directed to God for answers. Who am I? A redeemed sinner.

Prayer of Confusion

Will somebody tell me how to live? What is the secret? How do I give?

How do I yield my heart?

Will somebody tell me who I am? Which is the truth and which but a sham?

How did deception start?

What are the answers ... I need them now to questions I can't figure out somehow.

Am I wise or am I a fool? Am I loving or am I cruel?

How do I listen and who will speak? I feel confused and amazingly weak.

LORD, take control of my inner soul. Where I am lacking, please make me whole.

Search me and make me true.

For you are the One who gave me life! Tell me the secret, thus end my strife.

Teach me to live for You!

1982-1984

Narrator: As I prayed this prayer, Jesus led me out of despair and confusion. My request, that He take control of me and my life, became the turning point. Back on the right track, I still had a long way to go through the valley of grief. The following song tells the story.

Through The Valley

I felt so all alone, so lost and far from home.

I looked not forward to another day.

I longed for Christ to come. I said, "Please take me home!"

Then Jesus lovingly showed me the way:

"You must go through the valley to get to the other side.

It's lonesome in that valley, but I will be your guide.

I know you feel I'm far away, that I don't hear you when you pray,

but even in your valley, I am always close to you."

The grief I could not bear without someone to care,

though Jesus promised He'd be by my side.

I could not feel His love; I wanted flesh and blood

and so I took a road that led nowhere.

Then I cried out to God. I sought him in his word;

He said, "My precious child, you are my own.

You need to cling to me. Trust me to set you free.

Just hold my hand and I will lead you home."

"You must go through the valley to get to the other side.

It's lonesome in that valley, but I will be your guide.

I know you feel I'm far away, that I don't hear you when you pray,

but even in your valley, I am always close to you."

So now I praise His name. My Savior, still the same,

has led me forward through the sun and rain.

He's brought me close to Him. He's taught me how to win.

By trusting Him, I've learned to grow through pain.

"You must go through the valley to get to the other side.

Its lonesome in that valley, but I will be your guide.

I know you feel I'm far away, that I don't hear you when you pray,

but even in your valley, I am always close to you.

Yes, even in your valleys, I am always close to you."

Testimony and Praise CD 2007

Narrator: As people prayed with me and I studied scriptures more, I gained more trust in God's love. The love I'd had for Jesus during my child and teen years, which had dampened some, was renewed. I grew to believe God hadn't abandoned me as I'd thought. The next song grew out of studying the Biblical books of Isaiah and Jeremiah, which had become dear to me. It is followed by a praise song.

I Will Restore You Now

I love you so! You are my Lord! I praise your name! For you have said to me,

"I will restore you now. I'll build you up; I know the plans I have for you.

For you've returned to me, and I delight in you!"

Once I didn't know, once I didn't see that you came to this earth just to set me free!

Now I know that you sought me with your unfailing love.

With your blood you bought me.

You have called me by my name! You've blotted out my sins.

I love you so! You are my Lord! I praise your name! For you have said to me,

"You are my precious child. I love you so, my child. I will restore you now."

1984

The Sovereignty of Christ

You are the mighty King, Master of everything.

Though you are gentle, you rule over all.

Why do you plead for me? Why did you bleed for me? Why bother sending your call?

Your love has reached me and made me complete so I

couldn't resist all the love you did give.

Now I can worship you, Lord of the universe as in my heart you do live.

Jesus, I love you! I want to obey you and live in a way that will glorify you.

How can I serve you best? Help me to stand the test. Thank you for making me new.

You are my shepherd and you're my provider;

you have brought peace to this heart full of strife.

I will obey you, for you are in charge of me. You are the Lord of my life.

1985

Scene 10: Spring 1986. Woman stands on scenic bridge at a Bible-Camp-like Writers Conference, praying. "Please, Lord. I need to know what you want me to do. Is it wrong to remarry? Am I healed enough emotionally? Is it safe to marry Martin since he's been sober only a year? He says 'Can't we heal together?'"

Narrator: That night I dreamed that Martin and Jesus and I danced around in a circle together all laughing and Jesus appeared delighted that we were together. The circle widened as one or two children joined, then got smaller as they left, then came back. I took this as a reassurance that God wanted us together, and we married in June, 1986. It was a struggle because we both had so much growing and healing to do, and because the step-children were a big challenge with their own problems, but God helped us and I continued to grow strong spiritually. I wrote this song of thanks to God in 1999.

My heart can sing to you

You picked me up from my despair. You held me safe within Your hands.

You let me know how much You care. I praise Your name, Lord Jesus Christ!

My heart can sing to You! My heart can sing to You. Oh Lord, my God, You've brought me joy. My heart can sing to You.! My heart can sing to You.

Oh Lord, my God, You've brought me joy.

You are the Way; You are the Truth. You are the Breath that gave me life.

You called me close when but a youth, and taught me how to walk with You.

My heart can sing to You! My heart can sing to You.

Oh Lord, my God, You've brought me joy.

My heart can sing to You! My heart can sing to You.

Oh Lord, my God, You've brought me joy.

Martin and I had seventeen years together before he died of cancer in 2003. It was terribly hard to watch him wither away to a skeleton with skin on, but at least I had the joy of knowing he was a believer in Christ and at peace with God when he died.

Narrator: One day several months after Martin died, a song kept going through my mind with the question, "What now my love, now that you've left me?" It was a popular love song many years earlier. I decided to write Christian lyrics for it—turn it into a question for God. (Later, I wrote a different tune for the lyrics.)What my heart was really asking was "What shall I do now?" I had learned to trust God and wanted his guidance. I'd been a part-time freelance writer for several years and thought I should be able to do it full-time now, but I felt so empty, lonely with no one to love. All the children were grown and not close enough to give me emotional support. By this time, however, my relationship with God had become quite intimate.

Chapter Thirty-One

I love you, lord

2004

I love you, Lord. You're mine forever. You're my Redeemer, King and Friend.

You've paid the price; Your blood has saved me. You gave me life that will never end.

You'll never leave; You'll hold me tight. The devil's lost, You have won the fight.

What now my Lord? What shall I do to let you know how much I love You?

You gave me peace that I can't fathom, an inner joy in the midst of pain.

I want to be Your chosen vessel. "To live is Christ, and to die is gain."

You'll lead me on o'er land and sea. To be with You is where I want to be.

What now my Lord? What shall I do? A yielded life shows that I love You.

Scene 11: A woman works on her computer, stopping every few minutes to pray, "Help me not make a mistake. Guide me which singles site to use." She stops at a Christian Singles listing which mentions Agape. After reading a while she registers and checks out some profiles.

Narrator: I knew agape means God's type of love. The site had a Christian definition of marriage and some good devotionals for singles. I sent an email to Paul Vander Wege asking if he'd like to be my pen pal. We corresponded a few months, then I drove to Iowa to visit him. As soon as I drove into Iowa, I felt like I'd come home. I knew by now I belonged in God's heart spiritually, but also suspected I belonged physically in Iowa. The visit went well and we married the next February of 2006.

Many of my questions along this road, this journey toward intimacy, did not receive answers. But I do have some answers. Who am I besides a child of God? I am Paul Vander Wege's wife. He says I'm lovable, beautiful, that I belong in his arms. He encourages me in all my endeavors and says he's proud of me, so I call him my Barnabas. Most importantly, he allows me to pursue what I believe is God's purpose for my life, which is writing as one of God's spokesmen or instruments.

Listening to the NWC a Capella choir sing through my choral composition, "Blessed Be He" last spring confirmed to me that pursuing a music ministry degree at NWC is part of my purpose. I am becoming a writer/songwriter and ambassador of the Holy God who loves us. Why am I here? To glorify him by proclaiming his grace.

Narrator: The foregoing account of my journey towards intimacy with God was written around 2014. Since then, after graduating from college, I continued to write and lead Bible Studies and write praise songs and prayer poems.

In February of 2022, my loving and supportive husband, Paul, died. I rejoice in the assurance that he has gone to Heaven and that I will someday join him there.

End of Journey to Intimacy

Chapter Thirty-Tow

God's Paradoxes

The discussion in Sunday School class became heated: Does the Bible teach Egalitarianism or Complementarianism?

One the one hand, we are all one in Christ Jesus, (Gal. 3:28) with gifts we are expected to use (see 1 Cor. 12:1-13). Yet Gen. 2:18-24 says God created woman to be a helpmate for man, and she is to be under authority (1 Cor. 11:10).

We are to submit to each other out of reverence for Christ (Ephesians 5:21), and wives should respectfully submit to husbands who love them like Christ loves the church. (Ephesians 5:22-30).

This discussion reminded me of what I'd learned about a paradox, (this is "a direct but resolvable opposition between two true statements, laws, or principles."*) Even though these two viewpoints seem contradictory, aren't they both true? If God inspired them both, he must mean them both.

Before revealing these inner thoughts, I asked my husband what paradox he could think of. He said, "Well, I saw two docks right next to each other on the shore of Lake Michigan." I laughed.

A person might say, "I'm going out on the dock." He means a particular dock, his own preference or the one closest, but either is perfectly valid. Many times in scripture, two statements are equally true, yet seem to be contradictory. We may think *how is this possible if there is absolute truth in the Universe?* Our human minds think either/or. Yet the Bible says both:

1. Jesus Christ is fully man, (John1:14, 1John 4:2, Rom.1:3, Heb.2:14) yet fully God (Rom.1:4, Col.2:9, Mt.16:16).

2. God is Sovereign; everything is under his control (Pr. 21:1, 2 Chronicles 20:6), yet we have free will (Pr. 1:29, Psalms 119:30, Josh.24:15, Acts16:31).

3. He chose us (John 15:16, Ephesians 1:4, 2 Thessalonians 2:13, Mt.22:14, John 15:19), yet we can choose him (Deuteronomy 30:19, John7:17, Luke.10:42).

4. God wants all to be saved (1Tim.2:4, Is.45:22, Joel 2:32, Rom.10:13), yet few will be saved (Rom.9:27, Mt. 7:14, 22:14, Luke 13:24, 1Pet.3:20).

5. Jesus said God is Spirit and we are to worship him in spirit and in truth (John 4:24,) yet he didn't stop people from worshiping him in the flesh (John 20:28, Mt.28:9).

6. We are "saved by grace through faith" (Ephesians 2:8-9, Acts 15:11, Rom.3:24, 11:6) yet we must "work out our own salvation with fear and trembling," (Phil.2:12-13, James 2:17).

7. God's judgment is mercy. (see Isaiah)

These paradoxical statements are not inconsistencies. They are all true and inspired by God. God does not lie. They seem to be opposing statements because we don't know everything. In *Beyond the Cosmos,* Hugh Ross, PhD, talks about new discoveries in physics about dimensions. He said God, being beyond our cosmos, can see things through different dimensions than we can. We are limited by time and the three dimensions of length x width x height. But God lives in at least 11 dimensions.

Let's think of the "pair o' docks on Lake Michigan." If one wants to go on the left one, and the other on the right, which one is right? Doesn't it depend on where he's standing? If one dock has a fishing boat beside it, and the other is a sunbathing dock, the best dock is the one that suits his purpose.

If two women plan to go to a dock, and the two docks are exactly the same except one has a canopy, which one is best for the one who wants to sunbathe? Which is best for the one who wants to sit in the shade and read a book?

For the sake of an ethical example, say one dock already has a man lying on it sunbathing. To which one should the woman go? That depends. She might be right to visit with the friend or brother, but it might not be wise to sunbathe next to a scary-looking stranger. If she knows he is a nice fellow it might be okay if she is single, but if she is married it might not be a good idea. What if that man has flirted with her at work? Going to that dock might give him the idea she likes the flirting.

To apply this example to our discussion of paradoxes, whether a woman should take a certain position in the church also depends on a lot of variables. Each situation should be decided individually and with counseling. Yes, the head of a woman is her husband, but if her husband is in agreement with her serving on the consistory or becoming a Pastor and God has definitely called her to do this, then would it be wrong? On the other hand, if a woman is not submissive to her husband, (providing he loves her like Christ loves the church) is she likely to be submissive to Christ? And if she is not submissive to Christ, should she be on the consistory or be a Pastor at all? And neither should a man be a Pastor if he is not submissive to Christ.

Just like the "pair o' docks," there are so many variables involved in a paradox. We do need to study these scriptures and their cross-references, Bible notes, commentaries, etc. to try to understand the meaning of the human author in the context of his time, as well as the principle which the Holy Spirit is trying to help us understand. But trying to label people (as "egalitarian" or "complementarian" for instance) is probably not helpful. Certainly the Lord doesn't want us to hurt people's feelings or split churches over different ways of looking at these paradoxes.

Every doctrine of major significance in the Bible is clearly stated again and again. But for the ones that are unclear, it is okay to wonder what a verse means and disagree with another Christian about what it means, as long as we do so sincerely with a seeking heart, respectful of other points of view. God wants us to ask for wisdom, and seek the truth, but even more he wants us to love him above all and love each other. "Inasmuch as it depends on you, live at peace with all."

*p.64, BEYOND THE COSMOS, What Recent Discoveries In Astrophysics Reveal About the Glory and Love of God by Hugh Ross, PHD, NavPress copyright1999.

Chapter Thirty-Three

Love Itself

Before God was anything else, before time began, he was Father. He was holy, all wise, all powerful and ever present Father, the One who was love itself. What would it be like to have a father like that? Jesus knew. What was it like to live in union and harmony with such a father and the Holy Spirit in a place where no sin could spoil anything? Jesus did.

Yet Jesus—God the Son—willingly left that ideal situation to come to earth and take care of the sin problem for us! In becoming incarnate (becoming human), he was born to die. That was his purpose.

When thinking about the passion of Christ, which we do each Lenten season, someone might say, "Oh, that was easy. He was God. God is able to do anything." True, he was God, but he was also man and he died as a man. Philippians 2:5-11 says he "emptied himself, taking the form of a servant." He laid aside his godly powers to live as a man and die as a man—except without sin. This is the only way he could pay the price for our salvation. Only a perfect man could rescue us from the evil one.

Jesus became "sin who knew no sin, so that in him we might become the righteousness of God" 2 Cor. 5:21. What a trade-off! When he had accomplished this, he did away with the bondage of sin forever when he rose from the dead. It is like he broke the locks off our prison doors so we can go free. Now we can choose to believe him and walk out the door, or we can stay in our bondage. But he tries to draw us toward him, to convince us of his love and mercy so we will walk out into new life. Some don't believe they're in a prison and say "I'm not a sinner." But everyone starts out under bondage to sin, according to Romans 3:23. It doesn't help to deny the fact. One must acknowledge one is a sinner before one is able to respond to a Savior. But when we do, when we accept what he has done for us and in gratitude turn our lives over to his control, we are blessed with a wonderful relationship. For Jesus is just like his father—love itself.

Chapter Thirty-Four

Ash Precedes Joy

This week, I had the privilege of serving the body of Christ. It was my job to plunge my finger into a goopey mixture of ash and apply a cross to each forehead or hand presented to me and say, "Jesus loves you. He died for you."

An application of ash has been an Ash Wednesday tradition for as long as I can remember. It is always a meaningful service. But what does this tradition actually mean, other than signifying the beginning of Lent? Ashes have historically been used to express grief or as an external sign of sorrow or repentance. When ash is applied as part of a church service, it encourages people to examine their hearts and confess whatever sins they see there. Also, since it is usually applied in the shape of a cross, it reminds us that Jesus died to take away that sin. He died so we can be forgiven. Then, because of his love for us, we are encouraged to show acts of love to others.

From the time I was a child, when the ash cross was applied to my forehead I understood I was a sinner and that Jesus had died for me because he loved me. As I thought about that, I surrendered more completely to Jesus and felt great gratitude because he willingly died to take away my sin. The ash (sorrow for sin) precedes the joy of forgiveness and relationship with Christ.

Trusting God Through Adversity

"Before I was afflicted, I went astray. But now I keep thy word."Psalm 119:67

See also I Peter 1:7 and 4:12

Adversity comes to all of us. It makes sense, doesn't it, that adversity should come? After all, we are in a spiritual war, either on God's side or on Satan's side. Ephesians 6:12 says we are fighting against evil spiritual forces. Verses 13-18 list the armor we are to put on, and the weapons available for us to use.

Satan, is an adversary who contends with, opposes or resists all who are on God's side. God had created him as a good angel. But when he became proud and wanted to be God, rather than worshiping and submitting to God, he became evil. The absence of good is evil. Absence of obedience (submission to God's rules) is disobedience. So since he wanted to be God and couldn't, he became his adversary. Besides using physical obstacles, Satan often lies, deceives, tempts and distracts us in order to cause us to doubt God's love and goodness. His goal is that we will disobey God.

I used to wonder, *Why doesn't God shield us from deception and doubts?* In attempting to apply Romans 8:28 to this, I could somewhat understand how heartaches and pain could be used for our good. For instance: We take our little children to the doctor and let the nurse hurt them by giving them vaccinations. The good purpose is to prevent an illness. If a child gets a serious cut, although it hurts to let the doctor stitch the cut, this is necessary so it will heal.

Pain is often necessary in order to teach us to avoid certain harmful things. Just as a child doesn't understand why a parent stands by and allows further hurt, neither do we usually understand why our loving heavenly Father allows physical pain.

It is even harder to understand why our omnipotent God would allow Satan to take advantage of our weaknesses and our basic needs, allowing him to tempt us to leave the path upon which we had been following our Lord. This happened to me years ago. When I realized the deception, I wondered how a Christian could become so deceived. My motive was to do God's will and show love. Why would He allow Satan to lead me astray?

These types of thoughts can make a person feel abandoned by God. It may feel like all is dark and hopeless—like the light of our lives has gone out. On May 18, 1980, I lived in Moses Lake, Washington when Mount St. Helen's blew up, 288 miles away. The path of the ash fallout came right over our town. At noon, it suddenly became as dark as night and stayed that way. I wondered if the sun had gone out and if it was the end of the world. I actually hoped it was, because the "ash" had already fallen over my heart. My marriage was dying and I wanted Jesus to come and take me to Heaven. Of course, it wasn't the end of the world. The sun hadn't gone out. It was still there behind the ash. Eventually, the ash quit falling and God gave people strength to clean up the mess in our town. During the following years, God restored my heart and my life, too.

I love the scripture in John 1:4-5 which says, "In him was life, and the life was the light of men. The light shines in the darkness, and the darkness has not overcome it,"

(RSV). The word here translated "overcome" can be translated in different ways like extinguish or comprehend or understand. Jesus is the light that Satan can neither extinguish nor comprehend.

Jesus promised "Lo, I am with you always," (Mt. 8:28). Just like the sun may seem to be gone at night or when there is an eclipse, sometimes Jesus seems to be gone. Maybe some sin has come between to block our sight of him. Or maybe he has placed something to block our sight of him for the purpose of our growth or some other reason.

Only God knows why he sometimes hides himself from us, but it must be for our good as his Word says in Romans 8:28. "I am not skilled to understand," Aaron Shust sings in his beautiful worship hymn, *My Savior, My God.* But he knows Jesus is his Savior.

I know now that God is holy and righteous and he knows and does what is best for us. Therefore, I want to stay submitted to him, for if I get out from under God's umbrella of protection, I will be in danger of believing Satan's lies and falling under his deception and control.

Chapter Thirty-Five

How Does God Teach Trust?

As we "fix our eyes" on Jesus, focusing on Him and His will, we learn to trust Him. We also may learn to trust God during difficult experiences. A favorite song of mine says "If I'd never had a problem, I wouldn't know that God could solve them." (See YouTube, "Through it All.")

We may learn to trust God through personal encounters with him. Isaiah 6 tells of an amazing encounter the prophet Isaiah had. Isaiah saw the Lord as he really is, high and lifted up, majestic, honored, and worshiped. His reaction was to say, "Woe is me! For I am lost;" (Isaiah 6:1-5, RSV). Isaiah felt convicted. After Isaiah's conviction and feelings of despair over his sin, an angel brought a burning coal from the altar, touched his mouth, and told him, "your guilt is taken away, and your sin if forgiven," (Isa.6:7).

Saul of Tarsus had an amazing encounter with God, too. On the way to Damascus to persecute the Christians, he saw a great light and Jesus Christ appeared to him (Acts 9:1-9). This was a major life-changing experience and Saul became known as Paul the Apostle. Also, in my lifetime, I have heard of many encounters or instances of Jesus appearing to Muslims and others, and then they have become Christians with transformed lives.

A Third way God teaches us to trust him is through scripture. After Isaiah went through his conviction and cleansing, God commissioned him to speak to the nation of

Judah. Isaiah wrote his eloquent book telling of God's mercy and about the Messiah God would send.

We all need to be cleansed by Jesus, who died for us, before we can fit into God's plans for our lives. We learn from Scripture that, just as the burning coal did not destroy Isaiah's lips but cleansed them, God's judgment is never meant to destroy people but to bring them into right relationships with him. Judgment is not meant to destroy but to rescue.

Isaiah became known as the evangelical prophet because of his good news that God is merciful. He told Israel God wanted them to return to Him, to trust and obey Him and fulfill their purpose as His people. God wants this for us, also.

Israel as a nation eventually achieved her purpose: Jesus Christ was born of the Jews about 400 years after Isaiah prophesied of the coming Messiah. As John 1:14 says, "The Word became flesh and dwelt among us, full of grace and truth."

Prayer: "Thank you, heavenly Father, for teaching us to trust that you are a merciful God. Thank you for bringing us to conviction and repentance so we can experience you forgiveness and cleansing. Thank you for using our trials to refine and purify us. Please enable us to bear fruit in you Kingdom and trust you more completely. In Jesus' name, Amen.

Chapter Thirty-Six

I'm Going For a Walk

"Your cholesterol is high again. Are you getting enough exercise?"

I was embarrassed to tell the Doctor, "No, I haven't been doing my daily walks for a while." She encouraged me to get back to a regular schedule of walking at least a mile a day.

The next day I felt good about bundling up against the winter weather and doing my walk. I couldn't go far because of being out of shape, but I thought "That's okay. I'll build up my strength as I go out each day." The next day after walking, I realized I actually felt more energetic

However, the following day I looked out at the snow. *Oh well, I'll go to the fitness center later,* I thought, *or go walking at the Old Hospital.* As the day wore on, I grew tired so took a nap. Later, doing the work which had piled up seemed more important than a walk. *Besides, I'm doing exercise while I do housework,* I thought. Other excuses throughout the week also kept me from exercising. I wondered how I could get the self-control to overcome this problem. Would I have to get sick in order to want it enough?

In our walk with Jesus, some of us make excuses too. "I'm too tired to read the Bible." "I can't understand it anyway." "I can't find a good devotional guide." "My prayers don't seem to work, so why bother." "It's too cold to go to church today." "We need family time instead."

Then we wonder why our relationship with God is not more healthy.

What is needed to overcome excuses which are a detriment to our bodies and our spirits?

If we love our families, shouldn't we want to stay healthy for their sake?

If we love Jesus, shouldn't we want to grow spiritually so we can have better fellowship with him and live a more obedient life to his glory?

We need to exercise self-control in order to overcome the excuses.

Self-control is listed as one of the nine fruits of the Spirit in Galatians 5:22-23. If we are Christians, we have Jesus' Spirit living within us. He is growing the fruit in us. But we need to cooperate by obeying. The Bible says "I can do all this through him who gives me strength," (Philippians 4:13).

Another verse which can encourage and give strength to do what is best for our bodies and spirits is: "No temptation has overtaken you except what is common to mankind. And God is faithful; he will not let you be tempted beyond what you can bear. But when you are tempted, he will also provide a way out so that you can endure it.

These verses will help the one who wants to do what is right. But if we persist in excuses, after knowing in our hearts what God wants us to do, we are simply being disobedient and will need to be disciplined by our Heavenly Father.

I'm going to go for a walk tomorrow

If I Were …

"…justified freely by his grace through the redemption that came by Jesus Christ" (Rom. 3:24). Also read: Ephesians 2:4-10)

The trees are already starting to change to their beautiful fall colors here in NW Iowa. I love to look at them and feel the gentle breeze that makes them seem to be dancing. When I go for walks in the fall, I often feel a compulsion to pick up pretty leaves that have fallen to the ground. I choose the ones that are perfectly formed, with no flaws or bug holes, and a rich red or green or yellow or brown color.

I find myself asking my Lord, "If I were a beautiful leaf, would you pick me up?"

The question is plaintive. I know I'm not in perfect shape. The devil has wreaked havoc on my life, so the original perfect creation of me is flawed. I don't feel like I would appeal to an awesome, holy God.

Then, I hear Jesus speaking to me through his Holy Spirit in my heart: "Yes, I would pick you up. I have picked you up. You are my child and I love you. Besides, by my cross I have made you flawless. Your sin has been washed away by my blood. You are justified (made holy) in my sight and you are beautiful to me."

What joy these words bring! The song, *Flawless,* by Mercy Me, continues the thought.

Prayer: I praise you and thank you, Lord Jesus, for accepting me as your own and taking away my sins.   Amen.

Chapter Thirty-Seven

Empower My Words

Empower my words, gracious Father, that I may proclaim thy truth!

You who spoke and it came to be, you whose Word came to live in me,

Grant that the blind may come to see your everlasting grace.

Empower my words, Holy Spirit, to melt the hardened hearts,

Make my words like soft, gentle rain, cleansing wounds and soothing the pain.

May my message not be in vain. Please speak, O Lord, through me.

Empower my words, Christ Jesus, to show who you really are!

You are first, above everything. Savior, LORD, the King of all kings.

With love my heart, enraptured, sings to glorify your name.

Empower my words to speak boldly as Spokesman of your grace.

You who paid the debt of my sin, you who healed my hurts deep within,

Show me the best way I can begin to reach their hearts for you.

Judith Vander Wege